PEOPLE, PROCESSES, AND MANAGING DATA

Gerald W. McLaughlin
Richard D. Howard
Lore A. Balkan
Elizabeth W. Blythe

THE ASSOCIATION FOR INSTITUTIONAL RESEARCH
Number Eleven
Resources in Institutional Research

©1998 Association for Institutional Research
114 Stone Building
Florida State University
Tallahassee, FL 32306-4462

ISBN 1-882393-07-4

Table of Contents

FOREWORD

All data is meta to something.—David McGoveran (from a tag
line on the Internet)

Welcome to our discussion on managing data. Why are we discussing
data management? The answer is simple: We all make decisions and
often wish we had better data and information to make more intelligent
decisions. We firmly believe that at the core of a "quality" institutional
research function is the ability to add value to facts in, on, and about the
institution. We also believe that if we, as a profession, can develop a
structured management process, which adds value to the data in our
institutions, then we have identified a core methodology for institutional
research.

As new technologies enter our institutions, it has become painfully
clear that technology or more complex software does not solve the problem
of poor data. The value of data in support of decision making will only
improve when the data are strategically managed. There are key systematic,
sequential activities which must be performed to produce usable data; and,
the foundation of institutional research starts with usable (or quality) data.
It is these systematic, sequential, and significant activities which are
identified and described in this monograph.

Using Peter Senge's (1990) notions of organizational learning as a
backbone, the discussion in Chapter 1 is a description of the decision-
making environment and data use typically found at our colleges and
universities. In Chapter 2, a sequential five-function model is described
which takes basic data and transforms them into information designed to
increase intelligence in the decision-making process. These functions
require various activities, tasks, and events, which are described in Chapters
4, 5, and 6. In each of these chapters, a specific role in the data management
process is described. In Chapter 4, we describe the Custodian who supplies
the data. In Chapter 5, we describe the Broker who restructures the data
into information. In Chapter 6, we describe the Manager who supports
increased knowledge and accountability across the institution by using data-
based information in decision making.

Structured institutional data management and data-based decision
making will, at most institutions, require a change in the way decision making
occurs. In Chapter 7, we discuss some of the integral issues and barriers
to change which you may experience and we seek to explain how you
might deal with some of the individuals on your campus who may not be
ready to embrace data-based decision making.

Throughout the monograph, frequent problems with data management
are identified and some probable causes and possible cures are discussed.

The detailed steps in the management of data and the corresponding checklists are designed to make institutional data and information a strategic institutional asset. Our conceptual model, the Information Support Circle, guided the development of the data management processes outlined in this monograph.

The Information Support Circle was adapted from the scientific method we learned in high school chemistry. Ideas are identified, unknowns are established, beliefs identify testable hypotheses, data are collected and analyzed, interpretations are developed, and conclusions are presented and focused on a new set of relevant unknowns. This monograph follows a parallel process designed to add value to institutional data and information.

While the monograph is based on this conceptual model, the work has been developed from a very pragmatic and applied perspective. We have a combination of over half a century of experience (unevenly distributed) in institutional research. The issues described became important to us from a basic desire for survival in our institutions. Our organizational responsibilities have required that we apply various methodologies to support the management and planning of higher education. These initiatives were neither relevant nor rewarded if the data were unusable in the decision making or planning processes we were charged to support.

We started thinking seriously about the concepts of data quality some twelve years ago, writing articles, presenting papers, and conducting workshops on the topic. In writing this monograph, we have used much of the material developed in preparation for these activities, modified as we have learned. The following ideas represent a much clearer vision of how we think the management of data works than when we started thinking through these issues over a decade ago.

The flow of ideas in this monograph is designed to create a logical focus on strategies, which involve the entire organization in data quality improvement processes. To this end, we guide the reader through a sequence of:

1. thinking about the management and use of data;

2. considering the problems which may exist in providing needed information support;

3. describing the steps to create stable, consistent, and documented data;

4. describing the steps in brokering the standardized data into an institutional asset;

5. describing the steps in moving the data into production and use; and,

6. considering the processes needed to support the continual

improvement of data quality and information available to decision makers.

The ideas presented in this monograph are our beliefs, refined by applying the Information Support Circle to support systematic problem solving and decision making. We do not represent our ideas as the only way to manage and improve data, but as food for thought, hoping that we can all continue to learn. Bon Appetit!

About the Authors

Gerald W. McLaughlin currently is Director of the Office of Institutional Research and Planning Analysis at Virginia Tech where he has worked since 1971. He is active in the Association for Institututional Research (AIR) and has presented papers and workshops on managing data and decision support in IR to include presentations at the Basic IR Institute. He has served as AIR President and Forum Chair and as President and Chair of the annual meeting for the Southern AIR. He has also chaired the AIR Publications Committee, edited the AIR *Professional File*, and worked with the CAUSE/EFFECT editorial committee for EDUCAUSE (formerly CAUSE). His current interests include analytical methodology and decision support.

Richard D. Howard is currently an Associate Professor of Higher Education at Montana State University-Bozeman. Before taking this position he served as director of institutional research at West Virginia University, North Carolina State University and the University of Arizona. He is active in AIR and has presented papers and workshops on managing data and decision support in IR, including serving on the faculty Basic IR Institute. He has served as President and as Forum Chair for AIR and as Southern AIR President, Vice President, which included chair of the annual meeting and a Member-at-Large. He has also chaired the Professional Development Board for AIR and SCUP, and served on the CAUSE/EFFECT editorial committee for EDUCAUSE (formerly CAUSE). His current interests include the creation and communication of data and information to support planning and decision making, and the development of graduate programs to train institutional research professionals.

Lore A. Balkan has worked in the area of data management for 20 years. She is currently the Data Architect for the Information Warehouse and Access project at Virginia Tech. Prior to this position, Lore worked for three years on data quality assurance topics in the Office of Institutional Research at Virginia Tech. Lore has been a frequent presenter at the EDUCAUSE conferences (formerly CAUSE), has co-authored several articles in the CAUSE/EFFECT magazine, and served for three years on the CAUSE/

EFFECT editorial committee. Lore is also active in the Association for Information Technology Professionals (formerly DPMA) where she served on the national board of directors for five years.

Elizabeth W. Blythe is currently Project Director of the Information Warehouse and Access project at Virginia Tech. She has worked in Information Systems for more than 30 years, as a developer, a systems engineer, and a manager. Prior to her current position, she worked in the Office of Institutional Research at Virginia Tech for a year. She has conducted several workshops at SAIR. Her current area of interest is in providing easy user access to data through the Web - managing data, and transforming it into information.

The authors would like to recognize the work that Dr Richard Voorhees, Chair of AIR Publications Committee, did in reacting to and editing initial drafts of this book. His insights and recommendations for both the content and organization were a significant contribution and are greatly appreciated by the authors.

CHAPTER 1
INFORMATION AND THE ORGANIZATION

The second requirement of knowledge-based innovation is a clear focus on the strategic position. It cannot be introduced tentatively. The fact that the introduction of the innovation creates excitement, and attracts a host of others, means that the innovator has to be right the first time. He is unlikely to get a second chance. (Drucker, p. 117)

In all sectors of our society and economy, information is used to reduce the level of uncertainty in decision making. It is both an intuitive and methodical process by which more knowledge about the environment is accumulated. Our educational institutions are no exception. Higher education is facing serious management challenges as institutions cope with rapidly changing technology, a fluctuating economy, and increasing demands to produce more with less. These challenges change the way decisions are made, what data are useful, and what data are necessary. All organizations are challenged to create an environment where relevant and usable information can be accessed when needed by both employees and management.

Making Data Usable

The effectiveness of institutional research in supporting an institution's decision making depends heavily on the availability of usable data. Usable implies that the data are sufficiently accurate, timely, and collected systematically. The institutional research function is often called upon to provide data or create usable information to depict history, describe the current status, and anticipate the future. There are natural barriers which limit the value of data and information.

Data problems are mentioned most often as the major barrier limiting the effectiveness of institutional research and, as such, planning and decision making. Unfortunately, there is often a lack of understanding about the way that the data should be used, skepticism about the validity of the data, distrust because of obvious data defects or errors, lack of access to the data, and often only lukewarm management support for remedying these problems.

The most common factors which limit data quality and which have been identified over the years at professional gatherings of people who do institutional research include:

Consistency of data definitions. Limiting factors here include no agreement on definitions; incorrect interpretations; data collected in varying forms across campus; and, lack of adequate comprehensive measures.

Technology. Obstacles here are unsophisticated computer programs;

1

lack of tools to maintain, transfer and analyze data; poor data collection processes; lack of data management tools; and, lack of ability to support distributed decision making.

Data Access. Problems in data access include the inability to access data, and limited user knowledge about what data exist and where those data can be obtained.

The improvement of data is critical to the success of the institutional research function's ability to add value to our institutions planning and decision making, and is closely associated with many of our traditional functions. Years of experience tell us that there is no single best way to deal with the need to improve data quality. There are, however, some strategies which are more likely to be successful. In total, they amount to creating a data management culture across the organization.

While the data do not need to be perfect, they do need to be good enough to meet the needs of the institution. To achieve appropriate data quality, an organization first needs to understand itself. The discussion of managing data needs to start with an understanding of common problems that plague our organizations. All organizations are unique, but they do have some common characteristics. The stage for using data must be set in terms of the organization's ability to learn. As noted earlier, the use of data is a learning process. The ability to manage the information infrastructure is a learned process, and institutional research is a process of assimilating information to support institutional learning. And, as stated earlier, increased knowledge and understanding reduces uncertainty in decision making.

Disabilities in Learning to Improve

Peter Senge, in his book The Fifth Discipline, provides two views of organizations. One view examines the learning disabilities, which can exist in an organization. The second view presents the organization as a learning organization, which uses the knowledge it acquires to continually improve. Senge's organizational learning disabilities (discussed below) are extremely appropriate when applied to the challenges we face when trying to use data to support decision making.

I am my position. People in the institution focus only on their tasks and have little concern for how this affects other people. Data flows across numerous desks and functional lines in the organization. The registrar who only works to clean data for registrar functions will never be a source of usable student data for other needs. The vice president who only wants clean summaries will never be the source of high quality detail data. The department head, who needs restructured data based at the program level, has little reason to input better data into a faculty timetable system.

The enemy is out there. Each of us has a tendency to blame people outside our immediate unit or department for organizational problems. Since data must flow across organizational lines, blaming others for data problems is natural. If systems are put in place that allow and expect blame, then data will always be a strong candidate for fault. Since perfect data only exist as a fantasy, the means, motive, and opportunity exist for blaming others for faults in the data, and for abdicating responsibility.

The illusion of taking charge. Many of our reward systems require that the leader get in front and do something. This is particularly expected when an obvious problem exists. Every so often, there will be a glaring problem with the data resulting in situations such as people who are deceased being invited to the president's reception, some receiving several invitations, or alumni, who have graduated, being contacted and asked why they are no longer enrolled. "Take-charge" leadership to quickly resolve such problems can be disastrous when the take-charge person does not understand complex technical processes. While symptoms are addressed, the underlying problems remain, with opportunities for real improvement displaced by hostilities directed at shortsighted, reactionary solutions.

The fixation on events. As a continuation of the take-charge process, the leader is prone to focus on events rather than results. *Data management is a process* that tends to focus on improving ineffective structures and events. As such, it is very difficult to maintain the support of a sponsor or senior manager while continuously focusing on errors. The presence of good information is difficult to demonstrate as an event because it is simply assumed or expected. Furthermore, data improvement does not lend itself to being an exciting key performance indicator.

The parable of the boiled frog. If you throw a frog into boiling water, it will jump out. This, of course, makes some assumptions about the frog, the water, and the pot. If, however, the frog is placed in warm water, as the water is slowly brought to boiling, the frog will not hop out (at least this is what the book says). The availability of detailed data has gradually attracted the increased interest and awareness of senior executives to the point where data access is sometimes an ego trip rather than the means for better decisions. Substituting "detail" for "intelligence" often occurs gradually until the data manager is confronted with the "awash in a sea of data" accusation by those who suddenly realize that they do not "know" any more than they did in the years before the arrival of executive information systems (EIS).

The delusion of learning from experiences. "We learn best from experience but we never directly experience the consequences of many of our most important decisions" (Senge, p. 23). Some critical decisions are the hardware and software purchases made by the institution. The choice of a particular technology impacts many people other than those making the decisions, often several years after the decisions are made. While we learn from these experiences, sometimes painfully, we usually fail to apply this knowledge to the decision process. The decision process is often isolated from the experience.

The myth of the management team. Teams in organizations often tend to spend all their time fighting for turf, avoiding the hard decisions and avoiding things that make them look bad, all the while pretending to work as a cohesive team. This is strikingly similar to what has been referred to as the collegial process. For example, how many true team efforts exist between senior faculty and administrators? Yet data management requires the team effort of administrators and faculty. How many true team efforts occur between academics, facilities management, and financial administrators in a college or university? Yet these groups must combine management activities to capture, store, restructure, and deliver valid and reliable data. As we create credible data, the way decisions are made and the outcome of the decisions will change. This will ultimately shift the balance of power. Improved data is, therefore, a threat to some of the more powerful individuals at our institutions. This learning disability is the most regrettable, as it is the cumulative mechanism which allows and perhaps fosters the existence of the other disabilities.

A learning organization will not evolve naturally, but requires significant effort at all levels of the organization. The institutional research function is positioned to be an effective force in this evolution. Enhancing the value of data to create knowledge is traditionally an expectation of institutional research offices, growing out of a history of institutional research as a user, a producer, and sometimes the source of data for key institutional decisions. The institutional research function at most institutions has the relevant experience and expertise to meet the challenge of providing or facilitating effective data management to support the learning organization.

The Learning Disciplines

With the backdrop of the organizational learning disabilities as they relate to data management, consider Senge's alternative for creating a learning organization that would provide the foundation for meeting the data management challenges. The following are antidotes and vaccines for the learning disabilities. They provide a way to either eliminate the learning disabilities, or reduce their impact on the organization. The examples provided with each discipline demonstrate sound data management as an integral part of the foundation for organizational change.

Personal Mastery. Personal mastery is founded on personal

4

competence and skills, and extends to an awareness of the opportunities to evolve one's life as a creative work. Mastery requires applying an understanding of current reality to the shaping of one's future. The strategy used in writing this monograph was to focus on the mastery of skills in areas most appropriate to individuals working with institutional data. We hope this will help to identify and guide in the development of skills necessary to provide data and information as one component of a credible and stable decision-making infrastructure.

Those who would help or lead others are advised by Senge: "The core leadership strategy is simple: be a model. Commit yourself to your own personal mastery. Talking about personal mastery may open people's minds somewhat, but actions always speak louder than words. There's nothing more powerful you can do to encourage others in their quest for personal mastery than to be serious in your own quest" (Senge, p. 173).

Mental Models. "...the discipline of managing mental models— surfacing, testing, and improving our internal pictures of how the world works—promises to be a major breakthrough for building learning organizations" (Senge, p. 174). This monograph supports the development and use of mental models by presenting the process of managing data as a conceptual model having five functions, three roles, and two properties. We develop the five functions in Chapter 3 and the three roles in Chapters 4, 5, and 6. Finally, in Chapter 7, the two properties of the model are discussed.

We feel that the development of a mental model is itself one of the integral parts of successful data management. The refinement of this model comes after the use of data to influence a situation, frequently by a decision being made. It is when a decision is made that we see the value of structuring data to create information which is finally transformed into organizational intelligence. However, because our model is circular, the process is iterative. It is always necessary to review the process of creating the information and the usefulness of the information to the decision maker. Our model supports the learning organization precisely because it represents a process of continuous reduction of uncertainty and improvement.

Shared Vision. Shared vision occurs when multiple individuals have a deep commitment to a commonly held purpose. Individuals are bound together by shared aspirations. The best shared visions reflect, and extend, the visions of individuals. As described in Chapter 2, our vision for data management is simple: <u>Quality in our organizations must be supported by quality in our data.</u> This vision, as represented by our circular model, is quality through knowledge and knowledge from learning. The best management is a process by which adjustments and key decisions are supported in an intelligence-rich environment in which the focus is on continued learning. For a vision to be accepted, it must become a shared vision. Shared vision is only possible if it is understood to be constantly evolving.

Team Learning. Team learning occurs when there is an alignment of the individual team members in the process of working together toward the next higher level of awareness. There are three critical dimensions. First, there is a need to think insightfully about complex issues. Second, learning is supported by innovative coordinated actions. Third, there is a need to identify and use multiple tools for data access and retrieval. The roles described in Chapters 4, 5, and 6 are intended to support the development of teams, which function across these three dimensions. We suggest processes and activities by which teams can work to fulfill the necessary roles. Additionally, in Chapter 5, we identify and discuss various groups that can be formed to learn collaboratively and work cooperatively toward data management goals. In Chapter 7, a discussion of lessons learned and issues related to the change process, provides a background of shared experiences so that others can more quickly develop innovative coordinated actions.

Systems Thinking. The fundamental "information problem faced by managers is not too little information, but too much information. What we most need are ways to know what is important and what is not important, what variables to focus on and which to pay less attention to. . .and we need ways to do this which can help groups or teams develop shared understanding" (Senge, p. 129). Systems thinking involves seeing fewer parts and looking at the whole. By building on a circular model with the interlocking roles, we present a very complex process as a system. By identifying problems and symptoms, we provide a structured way of thinking about this system and thereby simplify it. There can be no quality in the management of data unless all the parts work together and recognize their interdependence. This interdependence implies willingness to adapt and to change, as does the Information Support Circle, continually improving and evolving data to intelligence. In the final chapter, we discuss change as a systematic process.

Institutional Research and a Strategy for Change

The institutional research function can be an effective change agent in a cultural evolution, leading institutions toward becoming true learning organizations. This monograph provides a basic strategy from which institutional researchers can influence the major stakeholders in this evolution through a process of continually improving data quality, extending and expanding the use of management information across our institutions of higher learning.

The management of data and the ability of an organization to learn are intrinsically linked. The improvement of decision making comes from the increase of organizational intelligence. The symbiotic relationship between reduced uncertainty and organizational intelligence evidences the need for a close linkage between the learning organization and the improved management of data. The management of data, as we think of it, fits the paradigm for discussing the learning organization. Unfortunately, the learning disabilities discussed above also fit.

Institutional research has an interest in the proper performance of key activities in functions which are responsible for creating planning and decision support information. It has an interest in the effective performance of the roles in a learning culture. Above all, it has an ongoing responsibility to affect change and learning by adding value to institutional data and information in our colleges and universities.

In the next chapter, we focus on describing the basis for our own learning that led to the creation of a conceptual model for achieving effective data management and information support. Chapter 2 begins with a basic view of the organization and the organizational roles that relate to information.

CHAPTER 2
SOMETHING NEW: MANAGEMENT INFORMATION

The critical issue is not one of tools and systems but involvement in the quality efforts of the business units. (Radding, p. 100)

The impact of technology on our organizations is changing the way we do business. Just as the automobile changed from a luxury to a necessity, information technology is now integrated into the way we manage our institutions. An IBM advertising campaign once called for "new ideas for new challenges." This concept has three key elements relevant to those who work with information. First, there is a strong theme of change. New is the norm and change is the standard. A second theme is survival in the face of challenges. The way we do everything is subject to question because our world is changing at an ever increasing rate. This theme acknowledges the ever-present threat that, if we fail to adjust, we will become obsolete. A third theme is less apparent, but provides the key to open new doors as we close the old. This third theme uses the word "ideas" to show that thinking is the source of influence and change.

There is the belief that change will come from creating vision and from new ideas generated at all levels of our organizations. We ask the people at the pulse of every activity to interact and generate innovative ideas. The necessity of acquiring new skills and knowledge is accepted. The ability to learn new skills is critical. Ideas are molded into plans. Resources are reallocated to support training on the new and improved practices and products. Learning from others comes by generalizing from their experiences and avoids the unwarranted expense of everyone learning everything anew in an organizational culture of "fail and trail" and "discover and recover."

A key organizational challenge is to make better decisions and provide better support for stakeholders. Information support must enable managers and decision makers to:

1. understand a situation and recognize the need to take action;

2. identify and rank alternatives considering resources, causality, and desirability of outcomes;

3. select an alternative, act upon it; and,

4. validate and defend the action.

The successful use of information for decision support depends on an information support structure that assures the quality and availability of relevant data that can be restructured for use by the decision makers. The

8

old ways of providing information support do not adequately support new ways of doing business. The disappearance of middle management, the development of intelligent devices, and the refinement of strategic management, are all components of the new challenge. To meet this challenge, we need new ideas about providing information support for our organizations.

Organizational Changes

There have been rapid changes in the technology that we employ to manage data. Complementary changes are now occurring in our organizations and in our concepts about information systems. We are experiencing a simultaneous push by technology and pull by management to deliver useful information. We have traditionally only focused on maintaining data in operational, or legacy systems which were organized by staff function: finance, student, personnel, etc. It is naive to assume that all required management information resides in these historical legacy systems, and that the challenge is simply to implement new technology that will deliver data on demand to an ever expanding clientele. Management's requirements are driven by new needs to perform analyses related to both long-term and short-term decisions. The operational systems that perform day-to-day transactions have not been designed to support management decision making, and probably do not contain sufficiently standardized or normalized data for the integrated, recombined, and longitudinal views required for analysis.

In response to the increasing pressures on legacy systems, existing internal and external reporting functions often use informal procedures to obtain data and interpret the variables. Often, there is not a predominance of historical files, census files, or standardized data maintained by the operating functions. In addition, there is often no formal assignment of responsibility for data management. The result is often a lack of policies to govern the processes by which those who manage operational systems capture, store, define, secure, or provide data and reports to institutional management.

Typically, when management requests for information fan out to different operational areas, each area responds by providing data from the perspective of its functional activity. The result is that: (1) the executive drowns in data with no options to analyze and transform the data to useful information; (2) the executive receives multiple, biased, and conflicting information; (3) the information is based on incomplete assumptions about the desired analysis and on data that are not integrated; and, (4) the failure to properly obtain the information produces organizational overhead, requiring the expenditure of extra resources.

Nevertheless, there are several organizational trends at many of our colleges and universities which offset the rather gloomy picture painted above and set the stage for creating a data management culture that can effectively respond to management information requirements.

The first trend is toward greater efficiency and competitiveness. With this comes a willingness to consider a variety of strategic alternatives. These strategies include changes in support structures, processes, and responsibilities. They also often produce an analysis of data needs. The second trend is the migration to new operational systems, and increasingly distributed modes of operation. New development tools, as well as off-the-shelf software, include structured methodology for building an enterprise's data architecture, data definitions, and standard code usage. Since these methodologies provide the foundation for any executive information system, the migration presents the opportunity to analyze management's information requirements. The third trend is recognition that there is a need for more participative management. (Harper, p. 10-11)

The use of participative management extends the number and also the skill-set of managers who need to access and use data from across the organization. It also changes the focus and organization of the data needed.

Decision makers often need an integrated view of multiple operational systems. This includes peripheral systems that are often not prime candidates for migration to integrated operational systems. This leads to the realization that there are ongoing data management activities that must be maintained to assure the availability of high quality information from all operational systems to support proactive decision making.

Trade magazines and journals have labeled these trends as "reengineering," "right-sizing," and "total quality management." Each term points toward improvement of the information support functions and spurs an interest in what can be done to accelerate progress. However, the lack of a structured process for coordinating various data management activities and relationships across the organization limits and jeopardizes potential momentum toward progress. Still, there remains a multitude of potential opportunities within the existing culture to leverage traditional relationships and friendships and to develop prototypes that push management's "hot buttons," thereby creating support for ongoing, quality data management work. Because organizational culture is dynamic, it is often accompanied by pressure to produce quick results that benefit the current culture. Producing relevant prototypes that address current needs increases the likelihood that quality data management projects will be included as part of other evolving organizational changes.

We can start with an understanding of the information support process, which focuses on the decision maker's needs (Table 1).

Table 1
Decision Maker's Needs

Needs....	Instead of....
• Tactics, techniques, and procedures ·	• Long-range plans
• Incremental changes ·	• Major decisions
• Majority of time spent on defining the problems, and developing possible solutions	• Majority of time spent on making a decision

We also need to define the authority and responsibilities of those who deal directly with operations and train those individuals to respond to opportunities and challenges based on the purpose of the organization, various alternative actions, and the authority inherent in the situation. Critical in this process are the acceptance and understanding of a conceptual model which includes operation functions, the process of decision support, and the use of technology which enables information flow. Equally important is the awareness that real progress depends on small incremental steps rather than large leaps.

Basic Concepts of Information Support

When our organizations were more static, information flowed on a consistent and traditional path. Management by evolution was perfected by incremental trial and error. Change was not anticipated and tended to evolve slowly, allowing the management culture to adapt slowly and comfortably. Today's dynamic organization needs a managed data resource whereby information flow can be adapted daily to meet current needs. We no longer have the luxury of evolving our information management any more than we have the luxury of evolving our organization. The future needs of the organization must be anticipated. Concurrently with the anticipation of new organizational structures and functions, there need to be new decision-support infrastructures. By understanding the steps in providing information and data, we can provide the required facts where the organization needs them, when the organization needs them. The old ways of changing the information support structure after the organization is changed will result in the data never catching up to a decision maker's needs.

We think the Information Support Circle (Figure 1) is a useful conceptual model for creating a relevant and sufficient awareness of these issues. As a model, it admittedly is a simplification of reality. However, it provides a basis for discussion of the process of creating decision support information.

Figure 1

Information Support Circle

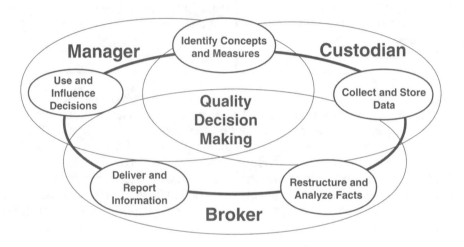

The Information Support Circle has five basic functions, three key roles, and two major properties. The five functions provide a basic framework for the tasks associated with helping people make informed decisions. The roles provide a structure in which specific tasks can be organized and assigned to individuals in the organization. The properties guide us in improving the quality of information provided to the decision process.

The Five Functions

The five functions provide a framework within the Information Support Circle for describing specific steps and activities (Figure 2). Each function has two sequential activities and a standard of quality. A short description of each function follows. Specific activities and quality standards are discussed in detail in Chapter 3.

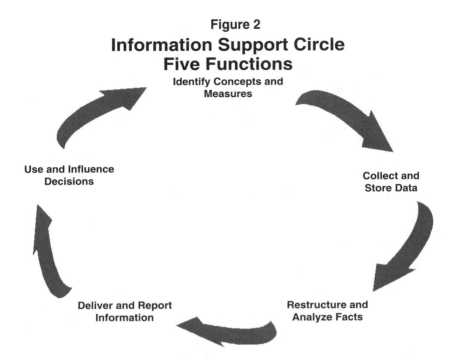

Figure 2
Information Support Circle
Five Functions

Identify Concepts and Measures

Use and Influence Decisions

Collect and Store Data

Deliver and Report Information

Restructure and Analyze Facts

1. **Identify Concepts and Measures.** Develop a conceptual model of the situation. Describe its major components. Include measurements which explain the feasibility of alternatives, desirability of outcomes, and availability of resources. Identify the key individuals and groups of individuals who have a stake in the process. Define the essential elements required to make the decision.

2. **Collect and Store Data.** Obtain data from various relevant sources. Include qualitative as well as quantitative facts. Store data so that they are secure and accessible to authorized users. Use technology where appropriate. Standardize the codes used and develop a collection of definitions and documentation. Edit and audit for correctness. Document the procedure, the situation, and the process of data capture and storage.

3. **Restructure and Analyze Facts.** Bring the data together from the various sources. Integrate using standard merging variables. Link to qualitative facts. Analyze with appropriate statistical and deterministic procedures. Summarize and focus the data on the situation. Compare with peer groups, look at trends, and describe limitations in the methodology.

4. **Deliver and Report Information.** Apply the information to the situation. This includes using appropriate delivery technology to make the restructured facts available for further restructuring. Interpret instances where there may be differences or gaps between the collection of the data and the current need to make decisions. Identify systemic sources of bias. Focus reporting on the specific alternatives and support interpretations of causality and desirability of outcomes.

5. **Use and Influence Decisions.** Use facts to clarify the situation, to make a decision, or to advocate a belief or value. Identify the way the new knowledge expands the previous understanding. Determine the changes in the environment and what is assumed about the situation. Consider the importance of new information relative to the issues incorporated in the previous conceptual model.

Three Key Roles

The roles explain the way the functions, described above, are related to institutional management. These roles may be thought of as clusters of tasks and activities that can be assigned. The roles bridge the separate tasks of the functions into sets of authorities, responsibilities, and abilities (Figure 3). The following are brief descriptions of the three roles in the paradigm. More complete descriptions are provided in Chapters 4, 5, and 6.

Figure 3

Information Support Circle
Three Roles

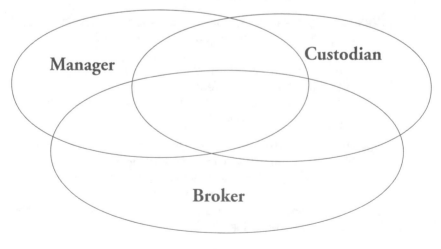

Manager

Custodian

Broker

1. **Custodian.** The custodian focuses on the integrity of the data and helps select appropriate data for the analysis. The custodian adds value by contributing operational knowledge. The custodian needs skills in the management and administration of data. The custodian also influences the selection of the methodology and the development of the essential questions which identify the information need.

2. **Broker.** The broker works to transform the data into information. This involves integrating data from various sources, restructuring data to focus on the areas of concern, and analyzing the data to look for causality, desirability of outcomes, and parsimony of elements. The broker participates and consults in the selection of the methodology and the development of the essential questions for decision making.

3. **Manager.** The manager takes the information and applies it to the situation. In this manner, the information becomes part of the intelligence of the situation and reduces the uncertainty of the situation. The manager is often the decision maker but may also be someone responsible for supporting the decision process. Some of the decisions are external, such as identifying what product to buy. Other decisions are intermediate and internal, such as evaluating business processes. The manager has a primary responsibility to identify the important elements of the problem, and also the unknowns.

Two Major Properties

Two properties provide a mechanism for evaluating the functions and the roles. They are the core values of the model, governing the essential actions: DO THIS and GET THAT. We have found it useful to conceptualize two properties although they are not mutually exclusive. Dependency is the property which deals with the influence each function has on the others. Cooperation is the property which deals with the relationships between the three roles. These properties are briefly described below and further developed in Chapter 7.

1. **Dependency.** The five functions form a circle (Figure 2). The value, which can be added for each function, is dependent on the quality of the preceding function. No function can produce quality or add value beyond the quality of the preceding function. For example, if the reliability of the data from the capture and storage step is poor, then no sophistication in methodology or increase in the amount of resources for analysis will overcome the low reliability. If the conceptual model is weak and erroneous content is selected for measurement, the resulting information will be seriously compromised regardless of the resources employed. The quality of the information produced is only as good as the quality of the weakest link in the circle of functions.

2. **Cooperation.** The ability to provide quality management comes from mutual investment and interaction of the three roles (Figure 3). If the individual filling any one of the roles decides to act in their own best interest, the integrity of the information support process is negatively impacted. In this scenario, the data custodian may change the definition of a variable to support a new operational need and inadvertently compromise the intended use in another area. The broker may propose an analysis requiring data that does not exist. The manager may start looking at new problems without notifying either the broker or the custodian.

Cooperative interaction among the three roles permits identification of opportunities to solve specific problems while positioning the data structure to support future needs. It allows the use of analytical procedures (1) to be focused on identified needs and (2) which are sufficient for the integrity of operational data. This synchronization provides the highest quality information to support the best organizational outcomes given the constraints of time and resources.

Changing Users

As institutions manage change, one likely outcome is downsizing. During downsizing, individuals typically leave organizations based on their readiness to leave, rather than the needs of the organization. Downsizing and rightsizing typically occur in the middle of the organization, the domain of staff specialists and middle managers. Further, reorganizing and restructuring often result in nontraditional management structures such as matrix reporting, task forces, or cross-functional teams. All of this requires individuals to develop a broader skill set. "Empowered" individuals need to be able to solve problems and recognize when they need to involve others in the problem solving.

The manager of tomorrow needs a broader and more flexible range of skills. This monograph helps meet this need in two key ways. First, a set of categories in which skills may be necessary are identified. Second, it shows related areas and types of activities that require cooperative work.

Each data management role encompasses a set of skills and expertise that can be brought to bear on any situation. The custodian supports the functional area. This requires traditional business skills such as accounting, personnel, and finance. The broker role requires experience with methodologies including management science, statistics, decision science, and computer science. These are the methodologies which facilitate the translation of data from the functional areas into information to be provided to those who apply the information to a specific situation. The integrator role requires an understanding of decision science, organizational behavior, and knowledge of specific characteristics of the industry. A manager in any of these areas needs to understand and appreciate the contribution of the others.

When institutional change becomes an identified need, reactions are often much the same as outlined by Kubler-Ross (1974) in an individual's acceptance of death and dying. The first reaction is denial that the change is required. The second reaction is hostility that results from uncertainty and anxiety as individuals admit the rules are changing. This is when cooperative work between units across the organization is most essential to both organizational and individual well-being. At the same time however, cooperation may also be extremely difficult to achieve due to individuals' insecurities. In this situation, quality information can be leveraged to bring the fearful together and create a frame of reference for ongoing cooperative work.

Changing Data Support Structures

The data support for the new organization will depend on the development of effective management data. This requires focusing on the decision process and on the uses of the data. Decision makers need an integrated set of data from both internal and external sources, including both current data and point-in-time historical longitudinal data. Since users operate in a variety of technological environments, the support structure must adapt with new software tools, expanded skill sets and training, and a new appreciation for the final product—management information.

In order to create a viable data support structure, the following will have to be developed and/or implemented at the institution:

Data Requirements

- Standard and integrated current data: selected data, defined and restructured to reflect the business needs as viewed by decision makers

- Standard and integrated historical data: selected data, defined and restructured to reflect changes, which are comparable with other institutions and useable in trend analysis

Software Tool Requirements

- Inter-connectivity tools: software to access and integrate the separate databases, which support multiple types of networks and is easy to use

- Relational and analysis tools: software which creates data structures and supports statistical analysis of the data, tabular and graphical displays, and "what if" analyses

- Security tools that are designed for a networked environment: software that limits access to sets of measures and groups of people

Skills and Training Requirements

* Skills: to analyze and restructure the data with the knowledge of the appropriate tools to use and when to use them

* Training and support: in technology and methodology (including statistical sophistication and awareness of the latest developments for data access)

* Knowledge: of complex analytical procedures

* Ability: to verify data validity and reliability

The Changing Institutional Research Function

Technical tools are necessary, but not sufficient to provide quality information support. The mission of institutional research is to enhance institutional effectiveness by providing information which supports and strengthens operations management, decision making, and the planning processes of administration. The institutional research function is most closely aligned to the information broker role and relates to data in three ways:

User. Institutional research is a user of all the critical and key administrative data elements. As such, it has many of the needs of managers.

Producer. Institutional research is a producer, dealing with data quality issues and data integration challenges in order to provide internally and externally standardized extracts of time variant data. This can be thought of as populating a data warehouse.

Supplier. Institutional research has an obligation to both its internal and external customers to supply current levels of information and analysis support while creating more effective delivery strategies to address requirements of various users of institutional data.

It is clear the successful institutional researcher is dependent on positive relationships with data suppliers and on the quality of their data. Simply put, institutional research is the basic process of adding value to the information and data available to a manager. Recent workshops conducted on effective institutional research highlighted four goals for effective institutional research related to data. These included providing accurate and timely data, developing a system of data collection, creating usable data, and providing trend data. Not surprisingly, participants identified data problems as the major barrier to their effectiveness in meeting these goals. Specific data problems include:

18

Data Definitions. Disagreement on definitions; incorrect interpretations; data collected in different forms; and, lack of adequate comprehensive measures.

Technology. Lack of hardware and software resources to maintain, transfer and analyze data; poor data collection tools; lack of data management tools; and, lack of decision support tools.

Data Access. Inaccessible data at both the local and state level and lack of data about the data (where the data are located, how the user obtains access, etc.).

To increase effectiveness, institutional research must support efforts to improve the quality of data. There are several reasons for this. As a comprehensive user and customer, institutional research has extensive data-use methodology skills. Further, those in institutional research can teach these skills. These skills include using statistical, comparative, projective, and qualitative methodologies. Also, as an office which often coordinates reporting with external agencies, institutional research is heavily involved in negotiating definitions and supporting the institutional reporting and information requirements. Standardization can enhance the value of state and national databases. When offering support to various internal offices, institutional research can often assist custodian efforts to improve standardization of data and definition of codes. This is also the opportunity to bring the manager together with the data custodian so both can better understand the need to obtain and properly use data.

A View for Adding Value

We have discussed the new management challenge facing our institutions, a sea change which forces changes in the way decisions are made. This impacts how decision makers are supported and increases management's demand for useful data. The institutional research function is positioned to be an effective force in the improvement of the integrity and value of the data and, therefore, is at the root of our institutions' response to change.

There is no best way to improve the management of data. There are, however, some strategies which are likely to be successful. The ideas and thoughts in this monograph are presented to help focus on some of these strategies. The ideas are organized to work through a sequence of looking at the need for improving data management, to describe some of the steps which we and our colleagues can take to overcome the problems in our data, and, finally, to look at what can be done to make things better.

These discussions challenge all of us to deal with three questions, which lead the way to knowledge:

19

* What do we know?

* What does it mean?

* So what?

In the next chapter, we discuss the five functions of the Information Support Circle and the problems, or "diseases," which are often associated with each.

CHAPTER 3
STEPS IN QUALITY INFORMATION SUPPORT

Strangely enough, it seems that the more information that is made available to us, the less well informed we become. Decisions become harder to make and our world appears more confusing than ever. Psychologists refer to this state of affairs as "information overload," a neat clinical phrase behind which sits the Entropy Law. As more and more information is beamed at us, less and less of it can be absorbed, retained, and exploited. The rest accumulates as dissipated energy or waste. The buildup of this dissipated energy is really just social pollution, and it takes its toll in the increase in mental disorders of all kinds, just as physical waste eats away at our physical well being. The sharp rise in mental illness in this country has paralleled the information revolution. (Rifkin and Howard, p. 170)

Assessing the Information Infrastructure

To avoid information overload, and the attendant mental disorders suggested by Rifkin and Howard, it is helpful to start with a set of beliefs about the order of reality. We do this with the five functions of the Information Support Circle. These become a means of structuring the information support process and the process of managing data. Before discussing these five functions in detail, it is helpful to realize that the institutional context in which they exist is unique to each specific institution.

The information architecture of an institution is the predominant style of designing and maintaining the structure of information and can be described in one of three evolutionary stages: decentralized data management, centralized data management, or distributed data management (Figure 4). Decentralized data management focuses on data support in the operational systems. These systems and their custodians are the source of institutional data and data definitions. These data primarily are used internally to support operational processes and decisions. The major issue in a decentralized environment is reliability: are data based on consistent definitions? Are they collected systematically?

Centralized data management focuses on data administration. The primary use of the data is for studies and management information. In addition to meeting operational needs, the data now become an institutional resource, integrated and analyzed for the support of central decision makers. The major concern in this environment is the internal validity of the data.

Those who create centralized databases must understand how the data are going to be used so the data can be prepared to meet the decision makers' needs. The source of the data often includes integrated census files taken from the operational systems and placed into a data warehouse.

Distributed data management focuses on the process which controls the flow of the data from source to use. Primary ingredients are the manager and the outcomes of processes or programs. Here, the major concern is the external validity of the data. To what degree can the implications of the data be applied to the current situation? Distributed systems include integrated census data which provides a campus-wide view, including department- or program-level detail.

Figure 4
Three Evolutionary Stages of Information Management

Distributed Data Management

Key Role is:	Data Management
Data Use:	Managers
Supports:	External Validity
Data Type:	Time Variant Data (Data Warehouse and Delivery)

Centralized Data Administration

Key Role is:	Data Administration
Data Use:	Brokers
Supports:	Internal Validity and Reliability
Data Type:	Integrated Census Data (Institution-wide Data Base)

Decentralized Data Operations

Key Role is:	Operational Systems
Data Use:	Custodians
Supports:	Reliability
Data Type:	Current Value Data (Snapshots)

It is important to recognize and understand an institution's stage in the continuum of information management development. The stage of the data management process should relate to the organization's stance. If the institution is operating in a highly centralized mode, the data management process should be focusing on the internal validity of the data. On the other hand, if the institution wants to provide adequate distributed data to a set of distributed decision makers, then the data management function must support reliable operating systems and an integrated census database before it can deliver data which will be of value to the distributed user. Clearly, the changes discussed in Chapter 2 are rapidly pushing all organizations toward a distributed environment.

The Role of Data

Creating and using information is the business of institutional research. Information has value when it reduces uncertainty in planning and decision making. The production of information is a cyclical process which includes identifying measures as data elements, capturing and storing appropriate data, analyzing and restructuring the data into information, and distributing and reporting the resulting information. The Information Support Circle (Figure 1) is closed by the user, when feedback is provided to the broker and the custodian about the usefulness of the information.

Data and information have value to the decision maker if uncertainty associated with the decision is reduced. It is almost certain that the more important the situation, the greater the power of the information. In other words, institutional researchers profit by the quality or usefulness of the information we provide the decision maker. More and more, our ideas and organizations will profit or loose by the quality of the information produced and communicated, internally and externally.

The development of quality information is a complicated process. This process requires that individuals work together with a sense of common purpose, an understanding of the information process, and an awareness of, and ability to use, some basic tools to solve problems. Below, we describe a process for developing quality information. This is an iterative process requiring cooperative efforts across the campus.

Barriers to Quality Information

As we have seen, five fundamental functions must be adequately performed to generate quality information. In the following, we explain what is supposed to happen in each function. In addition, "diseases" and their symptoms, that result in organizational disabilities which inhibit organizational learning, are described. These diseases limit the effectiveness of each function in the Information Support Circle and as such the quality of information produced. This "disease" analogy provides a model that researchers can use to evaluate the viability of each function in their decision support efforts. Remember, these are only the principle diseases, there are other related "ailments" too numerous to discuss. Although healthy signs are no guarantee of a healthy situation for a function, their absence definitely indicates a problem. We encourage you to complete the checklist in Appendix A. The weakest link in the Information Support Circle can be diagnosed readily from this checklist. We recommend an examination of the function with the lowest score since this function is the most debilitating. Be aware however that while this particular function may have the most visible set of problems, it may not be contain the underlying or root cause of poor data and information at your institution.

Function: Identify Concepts and Measures

The first step in the creation of decision support information is to identify the appropriate measures. The focus must be on: what information do we really need to know? and What are the essential elements of this information? Specifically, the requirement at this step is to identify those facts, both qualitative and quantitative, which are needed by the decision maker to both make and communicate the decision(s). The creation of quality information must be based on a conceptual model. This model includes not only the decision being made, but also the context in which it is made, and an understanding of the constraints and the consequences of the decision. The selection of the measure(s) must consider the key types of performance: effectiveness, efficiency, timeliness, and reliability. The context should focus on the ends, rather than the means. Once the process is implemented, measures should not disrupt the process.

Disease: "Belief Bulimia." The semi-random gorging and purging of data without identification of the concepts and measures. This prevents the proper development of a model and measurement of appropriate variables. Here, there is no consistent focus by the decision maker, so there is no way to determine a specific area of interest. After the objectives of an activity are established, there also may be a gap in their communication to those who are working to collect the data and create the information. Some goals and objectives may not be measurable using available data sources. There is no shared conceptual model of the situation and, therefore, no way to evaluate the usefulness of the data for decision support. The primary symptom of "Belief Bulimia" includes random interaction between managers, brokers, and custodians, which results in "knee-jerk" inclusion of data to address specific purposes until the next crisis.

Function: Collect and Store Data

After required facts are defined and operational measures are identified, the corresponding data need to be collected and stored by a unit or units within the organization. Computer-based data will be more accurate when it is collected at a single source where data first come into contact with the organization. External information should be captured in a systematic fashion using documented procedures such as environmental scanning. All coding must be done in a consistent fashion. Storage requires the systematic development and use of a database management system. In addition, there must be documentation about the data which is stored in the system. A data element dictionary and set of descriptions are essential components of proper coding and storage of data.

Similar measures should yield similar results. The data must be captured with the same set of categories and codes regardless of where they are collected, when they are accessed, or who is responsible for the data collection. Finally, the data must be internally consistent when cross checking codes. For example, an active address should only exist in the record of someone who is living.

Disease: "Data Dyslexia." This occurs when there is an inability to recognize data, often confusing one data element for another. Data coding often relies on an individual's memory, or is recorded on post-it notes, or the backs of envelopes, resulting in confusion about what is stored, where it is stored, and why it was stored. Concerns are often met with a "we-have-always-done-it-this-way" statement. The lack of a strong institutional commitment to the information support function results in the lack of policies and procedures. Resources are not allocated to ensure that data collection processes are documented and coding standards are in place. Traditional compartmentalization of units within the institution tends to reinforce activities in one department that may be inconsistent with the capture of data to support other departments. This environment is characterized by a lack of consistent technology and standards for the development of the data dictionary or other documentation. This includes non-compatible machines and multiple capture points for a given data element. All of this gives rise to creative data elements based on unwritten rules. One variable is used for another purpose "until later." For example, one institution coded people as buildings so they would show up on an annual list requiring maintenance because the people needed annual physicals. A readily recognized symptom is found in the statement: "This is only temporary. . .we are getting a new system to solve that problem."

Function: Restructure and Analyze Facts

Here, data that are originally structured to support operational transactions are restructured into formats that support the outcomes of the decision support process. Data should be summarized and analyzed so that interpretation and inferences of causality can be made. Data reduction can be accomplished by creating subgroups, combining variables, summarizing detail, and identifying trends.

Collected data are normally grouped by entities for which the data are attributes. Student transactions are stored in the student database, faculty data are stored in the faculty database, and so on. These data must be restructured and integrated to address organizational issues, and can require combining existing variables and creating new variables. In addition, analyses may be required to synthesize events where the summary of an analysis becomes a new variable. For example, based on a series of decision rules, an employee may be classified as faculty. This handling and restructuring of data may involve merging qualitative and quantitative data. Properly done, restructuring and converting the data into the users' frame of reference results in the reduction of the complexity of the data without major losses of relevant detail.

The analysis phase of information support reduces the amount of data to a level which can reasonably be comprehended by the decision maker while retaining the primary facts portrayed in the data. This step is critical to establish the causality in producing the outcomes being considered. This phase integrates multiple sets of facts. The process is rational and sequential, taking into account the intended use.

Disease: "Dimensional Dementia." This disease strikes when there is a lack of agreement on the frame of reference for analysis and interpretation. Should the analysis be concerned with one-year results or five-year results? How much data should be summarized? Interpretation is independent of the context in which data were collected. Summarization occurs over variables which have no logical relationship. Analysts use the most impressive statistics available. Data are segmented into groups without an understanding of the rationale for segmentation. Uninterpretable statistics result due to irrational data groupings. Those who suffer from "Dimensional Dementia" forget why the analysis is being done, data are grouped incorrectly, and the analysis is usually more complicated than necessary, adversely affecting the intended results.

Function: Deliver and Report Information

Delivery is the process of placing the restructured data and "cleansed" information in a location where the manager has access. Reporting is the advanced process of interpreting the information in context. Starting with the executive summary and continuing through the facts and figures, delivery and reporting should focus on the specific need of the users. The broker needs to provide support so that the manager can generalize the results of the data and information for various desired uses. The reporting should be structured so the manager can check whether the results and data apply to current and future situations. Reporting should allow the manager to determine how to use the results in a valid manner. To what future situations will the results apply? There should be the opportunity to integrate qualitative as well as quantitative data. Reporting should involve some basic consideration of outcome preference and causality.

Delivery and reporting can be heavily influenced by technology. At one end of the scale the broker presents the information to the manager, delivering an overview in person. At the other end of the scale, the manager accesses the information using a networked computer and tools such as decision support systems, and executive information systems. In this case, the computer/network presents the information to the user, but the broker is still involved in the modeling and analyses.

Disease: "Myopic Megalomania." This disease is characterized by the self-centered, shortsighted, delivery of data and information based on the whims of the deliverer or the deliveree. Reports are designed to demonstrate the technical prowess of the provider. The provider has an attitude of technical supremacy. There is an overemphasis on the media rather than the message and a continued disregard of user needs. Too much time is spent working with the tools, trying to make the results "exciting." In contrast, not enough time is devoted to ensuring the quality and relevance of the content. For example, "Myopic Megalomania" can be found when an Executive Information System (EIS) is constructed without the attention to the data management processes that support the underlying management information system.

Key individuals have a tradition of accepting information only from their own people. In addition, they have a tradition of rejecting any information or data which does not support their position. There may be a distrust of technology, or conversely, a worship of technology. Information is not available when it is needed. This can happen for a variety of reasons. For example, the user may not be able to specify or communicate what is needed. Or, the provider may not be capable of translating the user needs. Of course, there may be confusion resulting from situations where multiple uses are being made of the information.

Function: Use and Influence Decisions

Use of data and information requires user involvement. User involvement anticipates facts which are sufficient, relevant, and timely. The user needs to "learn" the information through a process which increases the user's "organizational intelligence." At this point, the information becomes integrated into the user's knowledge base and reduces his/her uncertainty. It can then be shared with others, used to make a decision, advocate a position, or refute an alternative.

A key part of the use and influence of results from the analysis function is the degree to which they change the way users perceive reality at the institution. The influence of data and information rests on the amount of change that results from their use, which, in turn, can increase the knowledge of the various participants and also help identify next steps, unknown components, and data needs. Together, these factors enable the user to clarify beliefs about reality; the way the process works; and, the way it should work.

The data and information must be structured to tie the results back to the conceptual model which was used to guide the creation of the information. The results need to be integrated into the thought and decision processes of the individuals involved in making decisions. Multiple indicators for a specific situation should give convergent results; however, they should not be redundant. For the information to increase the knowledge or intelligence of the user, it must be useful in anticipating, explaining, or predicting future events. As such, it must be related to the constructs which span the issues related to the success of the institution. The user must accept the information and integrate it into his or her knowledge about the key concepts. It must be sufficiently comprehensive to meet needs, be relevant to the situation, and above all, timely. Often, late data are worse than no data at all.

Disease: "Creative Carcinomas." This disease is characterized by creating facts, <u>as needed</u>, where festering sores develop around the lies. Specific facts are allowed to stand and interpretations are modified. There are conflicting purposes. Information that supports one manager may undermine another. Information also may be tainted by the belief that its source is unethical and cannot be trusted. This is particularly a problem for those who use advocacy information in a political environment. For example, if faculty salaries are used for getting money from state sources, they may be presented as low, so the chances of additional funding are increased. On the other hand, when faculty salaries are used to demonstrate institutional quality, higher salaries may be reported as an indication of higher quality.

Lack of structure may render the information useless. If the needs are not very specific, near random, hard to quantify, and related to personal whims, it is unlikely that resulting data or information will be of value. Statistics in the media are often "explained" after they are used. The response of decision makers is often "ready, shoot, aim." There is an executive belief of personal invincibility and skill. In this environment, there exists a tradition of blaming poor data to explain poor decisions.

A Checkup

As noted earlier, a checklist of "healthy signs" is provided in Appendix A. These signs were developed from items identified as issues which limit information quality, and were drawn from workshops we have conducted on data management during the past five years. There are twenty items for each of the five functions just described. This should give a good feel for the health of each function at a given institution. When we use this checklist at our workshops, the scores range from 2 to 18 with medians around 13 for each function. We suggest a minimum score of 15 to indicate a "healthy" function. This is probably equivalent to a grade of "C." Obviously, while a given function may not pose an immediate problem, a score of less than 15 indicates room for improvement.

It is suggested that the checklist be used with a representative group of custodians and managers. An analysis of all responses will show whether a shared understanding of the way various activities are performed exists at your institution. Do not be surprised if individuals think their areas are in better shape than the group does. After you use the checklist, focus your efforts on those areas having the lower scores. Usually, the lowest score will be the area which is the greatest limitation to the value of your data.

Role Interdependency

The quality of facts is dependent on the processes used to manage data and information. The information support process is circular (Figure 1). This process is only as strong as its weakest point. If at any point the process fails to provide quality, then the preceding steps will have limited value to the organization. For example, data are usually stored before analysis and delivered before they influence a situation. Because of this, the quality of facts in the one step cannot be better than the usefulness of those facts in the preceding step. As such, the function of delivering and reporting information is dependent upon the integrity of the collecting and storing of data as well as the restructuring and analyzing of the facts. The use of facts also uncovers or creates additional areas of uncertainty about which beliefs are generated. These are the beliefs which relate to the identification and measurement of additional facts. The reduction of uncertainty by the use of information generates the need for additional data and information. It is in this sense that the information support is a circle, an ongoing process, a necessary process if the institution is going to be a true "learning organization."

Successful data management is dependent on advocacy and leadership spread across the roles of Custodian, Broker, and Manager. It is predicated on nurturing new working relationships among people who previously did not communicate or were adversaries. What follows is a discussion of a strategy to increase the robustness of data quality improvement in the current structure while establishing the foundation for the new formal and informal structures needed to deliver quality information. This discussion looks at the operational implementation of each of the three roles: the Custodian (Chapter 4); the Broker (Chapter 5); and, the Manager (Chapter 6). Each role is described in terms of tasks, skills, and responsibilities. We also present important tools and concepts for each role. There is no exclusive linkage of tools to roles. Rather tools are linked according to primary interest. In fact, we argue that no one role owns a tool or area of activity. Individuals in specific roles, however, are likely to be assigned the leadership responsibilities for a group of activities and tasks while attempting to orchestrate events supportive of the overall, organizational data-management processes.

CHAPTER 4
THE CUSTODIAN—DEVELOPING THE DATA RESOURCE

What are the people processes that build in quality for the new corporation? It's the open, networked enterprise of professionals working together in multidisciplinary teams that cut across traditional organizational boundaries and that are externally focused on the customer. The model is based on commitment rather than the military's model of command and control. (Tapscott, p. 35)

The data custodian, or data supplier, is responsible for collecting and supplying the data. The custodian is associated with the organizational unit vested with operational responsibility for a specific set of organizational activities. The Registrar, for example, is often the custodian of student data. In a distributed environment, he or she may be responsible for the activities of entities which gather student data but may be totally independent of the computer operations. In this case, the Registrar will be the custodian of student data even though the computer center is responsible for the computers and the programmers.

The custodian concept recognizes that individuals do not own the data. They are, however, responsible for the data being of value across the entire organization. While custodians' specific responsibilities may vary, they usually include data collection, database management, and appropriate backup and recovery procedures. Or, these responsibilities may rest with technical personnel who are part of the computing center. Whether or not custodians are directly responsible for these duties, they are responsible for ensuring the duties are performed. This means that custodians need resources and/or the authority to meet their responsibilities. These responsibilities become more complicated as technical personnel are placed in different locations and the custodian lacks direct access to technical personnel.

Custodians are the essential organizational actors insuring the reliability of the data. They must control random influences in the collection and storage of the data that can destroy the consistency, the stability, and the objective nature of attributes being captured. They also are responsible for properly documenting the collection and storage of the data. Finally, the custodian must insure that standardized re-coding is used as part of creating cyclic file extracts of the operational data for inclusion in the organization-wide repository, or data warehouse. Custodial responsibilities for institutional data are part of management and frequently are delegated to system support stewards within a functional area or to a central computing function. These distributed activities are the basis of an organization's data management function. Obviously, the custodian who is lacking in technical personnel must be otherwise supported by appropriate technical and personnel resources.

Data Custodian Tasks and Activities

The custodian is responsible, and accountable, for the following primary tasks and activities:

Data Standards and Documentation. Custodians must work with the data management group and others to develop and implement standards for selection, compatibility, integration and accessibility of organization-wide data. They carry responsibility to incorporate and document these standards.

Data Collection and Storage. Custodians must assure reliable data collection processes, maintain a list of allowable values, and archive data at standard cycles.

Data Validation and Correction. Custodians implement and document validity checks and documentation in applications that capture, update, or report critical data. They develop and measure data quality and respond by repairing erroneous data, adjusting the processes that created erroneous data, and notifying impacted users of the corrections.

Data Security. Custodians should implement and document access procedures to provide adequate protection as determined by management and monitor violations. They implement backup and recovery procedures that protect against threats to data integrity arising from system failure, faulty manipulation, or other disasters.

Data Availability. Custodians provide accessible, meaningful, and timely machine-readable data which clearly identifies collection and modification dates and procedures. They work with central data management to provide training and consulting on data use and solicit input for improving data quality and delivery.

The Underlying Organizational Support

As we begin discussing data standards and data administration, it is important to understand underlying organizational structure. Standards must emerge from the various functional areas to be integrated. This effort should be coordinated by a central data management function focused on producing management information. As such, this producer is in turn the custodian of a central data repository which contains important parts of the organizational data extracted cyclically and stored in a standardized form. This activity

31

often includes running the organizational data warehouse with varying levels of responsibility for acquisition and distribution.

Establishment of an ongoing process for managing standardized data in terms of edit, validation, update, alteration, audit, correction, and distribution is critical to data management. Standards for these functions can be met where the institution creates appropriate conditions that incorporate the Shewart Cycle (Gitlow & Gitlow) for continuous improvement (Figure 5).

Figure 5

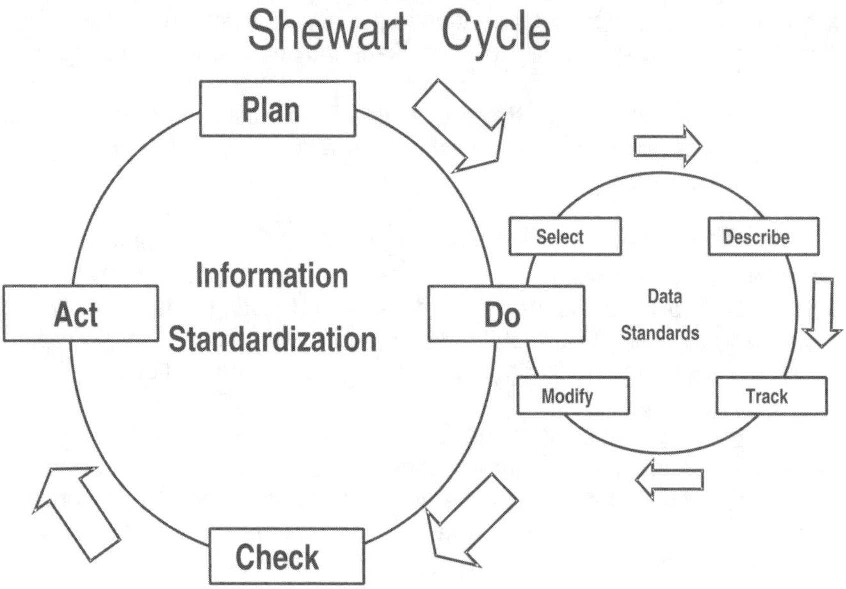

Shewart Cycle

The following set of activities (Plan, Do, Check, Act), structured within the Shewart Cycle, are necessary for the support of data management:

Plan—Data Management Structure

- Identify and establish an official source for critical entities with a list of standard values for key attributes (This is the beginning of a centralized data repository.)

- Assign data custodial responsibility and accountability

- Establish and implement policies that balance accessibility with security

Do—Data Standardization

- Standardize data descriptions, definitions, and documentation

32

- Apply consistent definitions over time (historical data)

- Cross-reference all occurrences of a data element across the organization

Check—Processes and Procedures
- Implement systematic edits and validation to ensure completeness and accuracy

- Establish audits for accuracy and measures of accountability

- Develop a process for reporting the results of the data edits, audits, and checks

Act—Implement and Monitor Data Access and Data Use
- Create query capability to identify data sources and data modification procedures

- Ensure the retention of historical data as well as ready access to timely and historical data by trained users

- Survey users to measure the extent that data usage is clear and meaningful

For these processes to assure data quality, all stakeholders—suppliers, producers, and users—must be involved at different points in data management processes. This requires that: (1) the operational offices supply reliable data; (2) the central data management function integrates and refines the data into a usable form and produces internally consistent information; (3) the customer has access and training such that they can generalize the information they receive to their needs and situation; and, (4) the three groups communicate, coordinate, and cooperate.

The Customer Driven Data Architecture

> *Architectures should be 'stolen', not reinvented...to the extent that data architectures are stable over time within a company, they should also be quite similar across companies within an industry. (Goodhue, Kirsch, Quillard, and Wybo, p. 25)*

As managers must respond quickly to change, they require data that can provide relevant current and longitudinal information from both internal and external sources. Accurate assessment of a situation is necessary to justify and formulate plans for change. Trend data is critical for planning and goal setting. Self-assessment data is necessary for measuring productivity gains. These data needs should be identified and developed into a data architecture that encompasses what the organization needs to know in order to do its business and remain competitive.

In addition to supporting analysis that blends data from the past and the present and anticipates the future, the data architecture must allow expansion and addition of functions over time. It must also be an architecture that can be readily transported to a variety of platforms in order to take advantage of increasingly more effective technologies, as they become available. Organizations with data architecture that is flexible and responsive to innovation are positioned to take full advantage of opportunities to improve efficiency.

When the data architecture of an organization does not support its needs, the results are rather obvious in that numerous activities are implemented at the last minute to get numbers and these emergencies seem to reoccur. The organization can respond in one of three ways:

Masking occurs when discrepancies or insufficiencies are ignored or massaged, thus allowing a weak data architecture to prevail and the organization to suffer the consequences of continuing to manage with poor quality information.

Coping arises when local or personal systems are developed in response to unmet information needs, creating a spider-web data architecture that fails to adequately support either local or enterprise-wide information requirements.

Correcting begins when quality data from the enterprise's systems are demanded and the organization accepts responsibility for stabilizing and strengthening the data architecture for the whole enterprise. The last response to poor data can be the beginning of customer-driven data architecture.

Today's managers understand the challenges of evolving data architecture, perhaps better than the traditional computer systems professional. Not only have the managers endured the unpleasant experience of receiving multiple and incompatible answers from their major information systems, they have also created their own nightmares. In their local or personal computing environments, they may have failed to maintain sufficiently granular data in terms of frequency of capture or level of summarization. Though few would admit it, most also have found it difficult to use data they have collected because of inadequate documentation. Additionally, these managers have struggled with data discrepancies for years while the organization's programmers cranked out code to process whatever data existed and considered their job successfully complete if the program ran without errors.

Those who manage a function or organizational event have a vested interest in the productivity of support processes. They are primary stakeholders. Their success is determined by: (1) how accurately they identify the customer and the customer's needs; (2) how effectively they meet the customer's needs; and, finally, (3) how convincingly they are able to measure their success and apply what they learn to further improve the process. While this view of success anticipates change, it also has a foundation of stability based on a data architecture that provides point-in-time quality baselines—or standards. Ultimately, the standard is really an outgrowth of information producers identifying and responding to customer needs.

Data Administration and Data Standards

In the early seventies, many information systems organizations created a central data administration department to help develop, distribute, and enforce minimal standards and to ensure that our systems could work cooperatively. Since most of these early systems were developed and used internally by a systems development group and usually for one database management system, the focus was on securing, cataloging, and standardizing database definitions. A data dictionary was often closely coupled and integrated with the particular database management system in use. Today, we are more likely to hear about Information Resource Management than Data Administration. The function of managing data now goes well beyond the initial database support function of most early data administration departments. The Data Administration Standards and Procedures Working Group of the Data Administration Management Association (DAMA, 1991) proposed the following mission statement:

- To combine activities, standard methods, human resources and technology for the central planning, documentation, and management of data from the perspective of the meaning and value to the organization as a whole.

- To increase system effectiveness by controlling data through uniformity and standardization of data elements, database construction, accessibility procedures, system communication, maintenance, and control.

- To provide guidance for planning, managing, and sharing of data and information effectively and efficiently in automated information systems.

This mission clearly has relevance for the information management issues we face today. It is significantly more expansive than earlier mission statements by describing an essential management function to optimize information resources. It generalizes to our changing organizations even as technology rapidly changes, users become more diverse and increase in numbers, and the information support environment becomes more distributed and complex.

It is also recognized in this mission statement that, while those who manage data must be acutely aware of evolving technology, the data management function itself is not driven by technology. In fact, the reverse is true. Effectively managing data focuses on building a stable information resource that can be quickly adapted to technological innovation. Moreover, with people throughout the college creating, managing, and disseminating electronic information, data quality must receive attention throughout the college. This attention must go well beyond control activity within the information systems organization and be understood and embraced by all of an institution's management. The term "data management" recognizes the fact that managers and technicians alike throughout our organizations must manage data and attend to the quality issues. Miselis (1990) makes the important point that since information is an institutional resource developed and used campus-wide, the management structure charged with ensuring that there is an effective and efficient use of computerized information should also be campus-wide.

Standards are the foundation of responsive, yet stable, data architecture. The essence of standardization is the adoption of a common language that enables shared understanding and provides capability to integrate multiple data sources. As such, it is a never-ending process that continually improves the quality of the information resource. The process of continually improving the quality of information begins with a set of values. Durell (1985) provides an excellent perspective on these values with "The Ten Commandments of Data Administration Standards." We include them in Table 2 as a guide, to help make us more realistic about our undertaking.

The Information Resource Dictionary

The primary tool to implement standards for a customer-driven data architecture is the Information Resource Dictionary (not a data dictionary). This dictionary should be relational in design and includes these characteristics:

* support a standard query language

* be compatible with transaction-based systems, and also with data migrated to the data warehouse

* contain a data dictionary which supports identification of common data elements across multiple systems

* contain meta-data (data about the data which describes a data element, where the element exists, how it is referenced, how it is validated, how it is stored, how it is reported or used)

Table 2

THE TEN COMMANDMENTS OF DATA ADMINISTRATION STANDARDS
1. The first rule is that there are exceptions to every rule. No standard is applicable in every situation. However, the data administration staff must not allow exceptions to become the norm.
2. Management must support and be willing to help enforce standards. If standards are violated, management must assist in assuring that the violations are corrected.
3. Standards must be practical, viable, and workable. Standards must be based upon common sense. The less complicated and cumbersome the standards, the more they will be adhered to. Keep standards simple.
4. Standards must not be absolute; there must be some room for flexibility. While some standards must be strictly adhered to, most standards should not be so rigid that they severely restrict the freedom of the data designer.
5. Standards should not be retroactive. Standards are to control and manage present and future actions—not to undo and redo past actions. In most cases, standards enacted today cannot apply to data design that began several months ago.
6. Standards must be easily enforceable. To achieve this, it must be easy to detect violations in standards. The more the process of auditing for the compliance of standards can be automated, the more effective will be the standards themselves.
7. Standards must be sold, not dictated. Even if upper management wholeheartedly supports data administration standards, the standards must be sold to employees at all levels. Data administration must be willing to advertise the standards to all employees and to justify the need for such standards. Data administration standards demand that programmers and analysts change the way they design data. Any lasting and meaningful change must come from the employees themselves.
8. The details about the standards themselves are not important—the important thing is to have some standards. Data administration must be willing to compromise and negotiate the details of the standards to be enacted.
9. Standards should be enacted gradually. Do not attempt to put all data administration standards in place at the same time. Once standards are enacted, begin to enforce them, but do it gradually and tactfully. Allow ample time for the non-data administration staff to react and adjust to new standards. The implementation of standards must be an evolutionary, rather than a revolutionary, process.
10. The most important standard in data administration is the standard of consistency—consistency of data naming, data attributes, data design, and data use.

- define any access restrictions associated with the data elements and who has custodial responsibility for specific data elements

The Information Resource Dictionary supports a broad base of users that includes data administrators, data custodians, system managers, security administrators, auditors, and end users. It plays a key role in promoting understanding of data across systems and organizational entities and in providing a central reference for data edit and validation rules, as well as other data standards as discussed above. The Information Resource Dictionary contains the entities and attributes from the source systems along with the predefined attributes and text from the custodians describing and defining the data. Dictionary entities include, but are not limited to, data elements, files, records, systems, programs, modules, documents, and users. The Dictionary identifies relationships between these entities, including predefined attributes of each relationship. This includes short descriptions, high-level descriptive definitions, and detail processing descriptions to support drill-down analyses in which data are mined from the general to specific.

An Integrated Tool Set

Clearly operational, managerial, and executive personnel must buy into the belief that improving data quality is worth the investment of time and money. We suggest investing in the following integrated methodology which produces a product that has value and can be marketed. This methodology is an integrated tool set (Figure 6) that has four sequential supporting parts: (1) People who perform activities; (2) Activities that utilize data; (3) Data that are manipulated using tools; and (4) Tools that assist with creation, reference, update, and deletion of data (Tasker). Each element in the tool set needs to be engaged to assure that the institution effectively manages its data and thus

Figure 6

Integrated Tool Set

Attributes	Support
PEOPLE & ACTIVITIES	
Custodial Accountability	Data Stewardship
Data Availability	Data Use
DATA	
Core Data	Single Source
Standard Coding	Archives
TOOLS	
Core Data Master Files	Library Archives
Query Support	Extract Support
Security System	

has quality information. The overall efficiency of this methodology in terms of sustaining quality information systems can quickly justify the costs involved.

People and Activities

Data Custodial Accountability. There must be someone in charge of each data element. This individual does not own the data, the institution is the owner and the data are a resource. The custodian needs sufficient seniority to make policy decisions about the use of specific data resources.

Data Stewardship. The custodians must assign data stewards who are responsible for data administration within a specific set of elements and codes. These data stewards assure proper collection, storage, and editing for ongoing completeness and accuracy.

Data Availability. The data must be made available, balancing security and access to all authorized users. This accessibility is the responsibility of the custodians, working with information systems and other operational personnel.

Data Use. Data use is governed by institution policy. The authority to change policy resides in the organization's management processes and transcends any given custodian. Coordination of data use policies should be done either by, or with the advice of, a data advisory committee.

Data

Core data. A subset of variables is identified as important for the management of the institution. These variables may number some two to three hundred out of the thousands used in the various operational systems. Standards are applied only to these important data elements.

Single Source. A single official source is assigned for critical entities and codes such as those defining a facility or department. A list of standard values is created for each entity which includes, at a minimum, a standard code, a long name, a short name, and a standard abbreviation.

Standard Coding. There must be a standard and systematic manner for describing, defining, and documenting each variable. This includes conversion to various coding categories and the mappings of various data restructuring based on historical activities and reorganizations.

Archives. Historical data files should exist and be accessible. These files should be time stamped for proper interpretation and use.

Tools

Core Data Master Files. The management data of the institution should be stored in a centralized database for authorized use. This database should have a data dictionary and be accessible by multiple users.

Library Archives. Historical data need to be stored in an accessible database structure. Crosswalk tables should be available in the same structure that reflects changes in official coding over time.

Query Support. Various languages should support generalized queries of the availability and interpretation of the data stored in the centralized database.

Extract Support. Procedures should exist for the extraction of data from various repositories and databases. This extract capacity should include the ability to select either subsets of data or to focus on specific variables. Also, extract procedures should include the ability to move data into various mainframe, server, and desktop environments.

Security System. The data should have subset, variable, and user-identification security capability. The security should be consistent with that used for non-computerized files. Access should be the default.

Standardization and a Centralized Administrative Database

A centralized administrative database (Figure 7) referred to as the ADB (Administrative Database) contains elements which are the core data important to the operations of the institution. Specifically, an element is included in the ADB if it meets any one of the following criteria:

- It is relevant to planning, managing, operating, or auditing major administrative functions.

- It is referenced or required for use by more than one organizational

Figure 7

Institutional Administrative Data Management Infrastructure

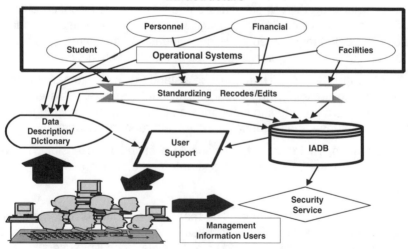

40

unit. Data elements that are used internally by a single department or office, are not typically part of the ADB.

* It is included in an official institutional administrative report or survey.

* It is used to derive an element which meets the criteria above.

Data elements, which meet at least one of these criteria for inclusion, become a resource for the management of the institution. A data custodian, a data steward, or a user may identify them for inclusion. At times, a process of resolving disagreements will be required, as the inclusion of a data element in the ADB will often place additional responsibilities on the custodian and result in the loss of some autonomy in handling the data element and its codes.

Key variables are an important component of the ADB. These are the variables which are used to link databases. They typically include such elements as an official building number, a personal identification number, or a course identifier, which can be used to link student and instructor for a specific instructional activity. Key variables should have a standard code, a standard long name, a standard short name, and a standard abbreviation. Every occurrence of the key variable should contain one or more of these attributes. Aliases should never be defined as key variables.

For example, in addition to the standard code, standard long name, standard short name, and standard abbreviation, the Facilities Master File of the ADB can include other attributes required by other organizational units. These are included elements required to check consistency with other data sources and elements required to maintain historical representation such as status flags, begin dates, and end dates. Master files like the Facilities Master File should be accessible and readily available to anyone with a need to know the information. The master files should include general information about each element, a definition for data processing each element, and documentation for assigning and maintaining each data element and its attributes. The custodian should be given the resources necessary to maintain the Master Files in their care. This responsibility includes developing procedures for:

* Maintenance of data items in the Master File to include editing and auditing the data

* Information dissemination about changes and updates in the Master File

* Implementation of procedures for archiving information from the Master File to include census extracts with time-date identification

* Coordination of changes, additions, and deletions to the key variables and codes

A Prototype for Standardization

The events outlined above require time and effort to achieve. Furthermore, they depend on the interaction and cooperation of numerous individuals who are not accustomed to working with each other. The best way to develop momentum across the campus for these events is to do a prototype project. The following is a description of a prototype project completed for the development and implementation of standards on facilities data and information.

The data custodial office, Facilities Planning and Construction, was involved throughout the process. The data custodian and data steward participated in each of the following steps of the iterative—Plan, Do, Check, Act—quality improvement cycle:

- Identify critical and key university elements and codes—Plan.

- Define and document data elements and related codes—Do.

- Measure and verify data and code quality and integrity—Check.

The first result of executing this cycle was a draft of a Facility Master File, which is the official source of facilities data. The Facility Master File contained: (1) Key Variables—the data elements that provide validation and translate capability; and, (2) University Core Data—the data which are required to answer university-wide questions and should be generally available from a central data source, in this case the ADB. This prototype provided a basis for the next steps in the development of an institution-wide data warehouse (Act).

Making the Custodial Job a Success

If you find yourself taking on the responsibilities of a Custodian, the discussion above outlines the specific tasks that you will ultimately be held accountable for completing. To facilitate the accomplishment of these tasks, you may want to check the degree to which the data and data management function is meeting customer needs and then set priorities to meet these needs. In addition, review data management policies, procedures, and existing priorities with the data stewards and clarify those which are unclear and develop new ones where needed. Technical shortcomings need to be identified and rectified as soon as possible. Look to colleagues at other institutions or in professional organizations for tools and technology that have worked in settings like yours, and, finally, join one or two technical groups such as EDUCAUSE or the Association for Information Technology Professionals to stay up-to-date with technical developments.

As an organization develops and refines the roles of the custodian, with the central coordination and implementation of standards, the key parts of the centralized management database will increase in value. The use of the tool kit needs to occur with the assignment of custodial and steward responsibilities. The creation of the architecture and standards should be consistent with The Ten Commandments (Table 2). As the custodian improves the process of capturing and storing the data, the broker will have more opportunity to add value to the data. The broker's role is described in the next chapter.

CHAPTER 5
THE BROKER—TRANSFORMING DATA INTO INFORMATION

One of the most difficult leadership challenges is deciding when to stop formulating strategy and begin executing it. Although many executives are action-oriented, the computer has increased our fascination with data and our ability to manipulate data. Top management teams now have access to voluminous performance statistics, market research reports, and other business information. In many cases, these data seem to hold senior management spellbound. Couple this data overload with even more sophisticated techniques of financial analysis and you have the "analysis paralysis" strategy trap—the inability or unwillingness of executives to take decisive action. (Stringer, p. 77)

The data in the university's transaction systems must be transformed and analyzed before it is useful in decision making. Managers can easily become trapped by the "analysis paralysis," described above, if they are bombarded with volumes of data that have not undergone systematic analysis and refinement. The way to avoid analysis paralysis is to have an effective broker function. After the data are standardized and stored in the core master files of the institution, they need to be restructured and often merged with other data—the role of the broker.

The data broker obtains data from various data sources and transforms them into information. The broker adds value by using structured procedures to give the raw data meaning in the context of management needs. The broker is often someone in the institution who is performing a traditional institutional research activity of analyzing data and developing useful management reports. This requires the ability to interpret the data and determine the type of analysis needed. This may also involve restructuring the data to make it more consistent with the business rules of the institution. The basic steps involve accessing the data, aggregating and summarizing them, merging them with other data, sub-setting and creating appropriate variables, and making the results available in forms which range from a subset or extract of the database to a highly summarized and possibly synthesized performance indicator report. Success depends on coordinating the data management functions.

Coordinating Data Management Functions

Brokers require support from the institution to be successful. Those functions that need the broker's involvement are defined below:

Information Planning

- Works with operational area managers or custodians, data stewards, and distributed users to maintain and share a model of the data elements and their attributes important to the organization (the Core Master Files).

- Helps anticipate and respond to users' changing information needs. The collection of new data or the modification of existing data takes time and is best done in a rational systematic fashion. If changes in data elements required to support key decisions can be anticipated, "panic" can often be avoided.

- Coordinates policies for the population and use of longitudinal data in the institution's data warehouse or central store of core data. A key issue involves balancing access with security. A general rule is that the restriction of data limits knowledge and is not desirable. No data should be restricted without a legitimate reason.

Standards Administration

- Develops and coordinates the implementation of standards for the data elements and codes in the warehouse. There should be a code for each data element. The code should be one of the predefined allowable codes, and should be consistent with other codes. For example, each student should have a code for "home state," this home state code should be one of the allowable state codes, and those students from the institution's state should be paying in-state fees.

- Works with distributed users, operational area managers, and information technology personnel to establish and implement data management policies. These policies could identify the organizational units responsible for editing the data, changing passwords, and correcting errors. These policies could specify the procedures for adding new elements and codes.

- Provides standards and appropriate documentation for use by EDP audits. This includes steps taken to secure institutional performance data in compliance with federal and state laws. This also includes disaster recovery plans, and procedures used to ensure data integrity, such as backup and recovery.

- Maintains an inventory of official code definitions and values for standardized data. This inventory is used by custodians to ensure that standardized data are populated in the data warehouse. These codes need to be archived. Processes need to be developed for changes in allowable codes and, as such, each code must have a start and end date.

Operational System Management Support

- Assists custodians of operational systems in extracting, standardizing, and providing data for the data warehouse. Timing is critical. Procedures should be similar across operational systems even if the operational systems reside on different platforms and in a variety of database management systems.

- Assists managers of operational systems in developing and maintaining data elements and definitions. This should involve some institutional standard for entering, updating, and distributing data about data (meta-data).

- Provides limited training and advice to operational managers about developing and preparing individuals for data management. This could include an orientation session, an electronic forum for sharing information, and a hot line for help. It is critical that the custodians and stewards feel comfortable making quality improvement suggestions to the broker and the manager.

- Helps operational managers create and coordinate user groups. These groups are key to rapid and effective communication about ways to add value to the data. User groups also provide and legitimize advocacy for change and promote shared discovery and learning.

Administrative Services

- Coordinates the identification of issues and strategies for dealing with data and information management. This positions the data management function strategically, allowing it to manage change rather than simply react to problems.

- Supports a process that improves data quality with a baseline of standards and measures of improvement. The interest of the key stakeholders usually will focus on current hot topics. If a topic involves improvements in effectiveness or efficiencies, the manager can show how improvements can sustain executive interest.

- Organizes and provides administrative support to an information policy steering group which includes personnel from the information technology function, the central data management function, operational area managers, system support stewards, and distributed decision makers or users.

- Organizes and provides training and administrative support to distributed decision makers who wish to use data that are in the

46

data warehouse. This may involve some training in the use of data and/or information in decision making.

- Leads focused cross-functional projects on data quality improvement.

Data Administration

- Manages the data warehouse, serving as custodian and system steward for the warehouse. The task of designing and loading data into a data warehouse requires understanding and documenting the business rules. It also involves the creation of new "business-oriented" data elements, and the creation of meta-data. The data warehouse is actually a collection of master files that requires custodian and steward support.

- Supports creation of a consistent and usable set of data warehouse data elements. This requires a standard process for managing changes in codes and data elements.

- Where necessary, mediates user and operational area custodial concerns about codes and data definitions. These groups have different responsibilities within the institution. They have different professional skills and values. As they act in their own best interests, conflict will result and require resolution.

- Distributes information about the data warehouse and its use. Educates customers and potential customers about its availability and value.

- Ensures proper archiving and protection of historical data in the warehouse. This results in the ability to use standard data over time. It involves ensuring that historical data are accessible. Information about accessing historical data should be part of the meta-data.

- Acts as the official source of the audit trail which delineates changing codes and data element descriptions for elements in the data warehouse. Detail should be accessible to at least one level below the current definitions and values.

- Maintains all information management policies. Since these documents are specific to organizational units, they need to be updated as individuals and units change. Management policies will also change as technology changes and should be reviewed annually.

End User Support

- Uses the data warehouse to respond to user requests and develops useable prototypes. A log of ad hoc requests to track emerging needs should also be maintained.

- Helps communicate users' information requirements to management and to the operational areas. User requests can be combined when users need similar support.

- Supports users' needs to integrate locally maintained data with the data in the data warehouse. This requires creating data set extracts, often supplying them to users.

- Assists with migration of users' local data to the data warehouse when it is relevant to activities, analyses, or reporting that crosses functional boundaries. Student outcomes assessment activities may require mailing addresses from the Alumni Association. These same mailing records may also be needed by departments wishing to form advisory councils. When multiple groups need the same set of data, steps need to be taken to integrate it into the data warehouse.

Technical Development

- Works with operational area managers or custodians, system support stewards, and end users to clarify technical needs. The institution can profit from having similar users using similar tools.

- Supports the information technology department in the development, purchase, and use of prototype tools and products for managing and delivering data. This provides user input to the selection of tools. It also allows for the investigation of prototypes by those with a vested interest in learning how a tool can help add value to data.

- Acts as a clearinghouse for data management tools and related technology. This activity includes shared learning with similar functions at other institutions and businesses.

The Data Warehouse

"Legacy" systems challenge data management. Old systems often use different database structures, run on different hardware platforms, and are under the control of many different areas of the organization. Underfunded and under fire, data management has not been a story of successes during the past decade. Faced with these challenges, Bill Inmon (1993) developed the concept of the data warehouse in the early 1990's to solve some of these problems. The characteristics of the data elements found in databases are presented along with the relationship of the data warehouse to other primary databases (Figure 8).

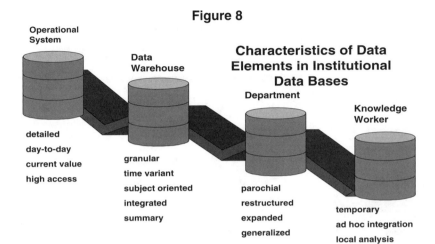

Figure 8

Characteristics of Data Elements in Institutional Data Bases

Operational System
- detailed
- day-to-day
- current value
- high access

Data Warehouse
- granular
- time variant
- subject oriented
- integrated
- summary

Department
- parochial
- restructured
- expanded
- generalized

Knowledge Worker
- temporary
- ad hoc integration
- local analysis
- PC based

A data warehouse is a collection of data from many systems brought together to support the needs of management. It is a "user friendly" version of the institutional research collection of census-date data sets. The data warehouse provides a "business view" of the data, and addresses the following problems with legacy systems:

Data Access. Access to data is difficult in legacy systems due to lack of documentation and definitions, complex security, and differences in the hardware and software environments of the source systems.

Data Integration. Data integration is difficult because of the lack of standard codes for university-wide use, different edit and audit criteria, and the different time cycles for extracts. Data integration can also be difficult because organizational factions prevent its use as a university resource.

Data Availability. Data availability is often inconsistent. Definitions differ across various systems. Both the systems and the management needs are constantly changing, usually independent of each other.

Data Integrity. The volatile nature of transaction-oriented operational systems, coupled with the lack of code standardization, contributes to significant challenges to data integrity.

Characteristics of the Data Warehouse

The data warehouse (Figure 9) is always physically separate from the application or operational databases. It is designed to support information inquiry and analytical processing. Elements in the data warehouse should reflect the characteristics defined below.

49

Figure 9

Characteristics of a Data Warehouse

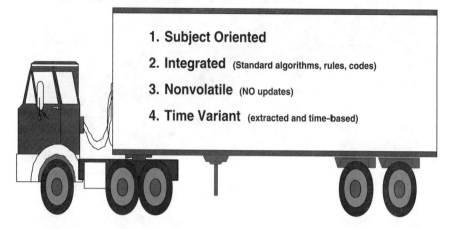

1. **Subject Oriented**

2. **Integrated** (Standard algorithms, rules, codes)

3. **Nonvolatile** (NO updates)

4. **Time Variant** (extracted and time-based)

Subject Oriented. The data in legacy systems are frequently organized around the application or transaction. Student data are organized by administrative processes or applications, such as admissions, registration, or student accounts. A subject orientation might be a student, a course, or a faculty. This begins to pull operational data together with a business view that supports management requests for such things as faculty workload projections.

Integrated. Integration is the most important aspect of the data warehouse. It is critical to virtually any analysis. It is also the most difficult and time-consuming aspect of building a warehouse. Integration requires consistency in naming conventions, coding structures, and in physical attributes. Over the years, application systems have been designed for specific functions, in specific areas, with little thought given to other related units. Data elements that are used in multiple areas commonly have completely different coding schemes. The warehouse brings together data extracts from various systems and translates the data into a single entity. A single coding scheme must be chosen for the warehouse, while allowing individual operating systems to continue to use their own schemes. Integration requires checks for consistency. An example of the need to integrate the data by subject is the development of data to support research about students, which involves class performance related to faculty characteristics over a time period of several years. While the unit of interest is the student, student data, curricular data, and faculty data need to be integrated. With independent legacy systems, the project would be a daunting undertaking. In a properly constructed data warehouse, the data would already be integrated.

Nonvolatile. Application or operational systems are continually changing to reflect the most recent transaction. Operational transaction systems are designed to answer the questions: Where do we stand right now? or What is the most recent event that has occurred? The characteristics, codes, attributes, and other data characteristics are very temporary or volatile. In the data warehouse, snapshots of data are maintained for a length of time. This length of time is determined in a tradeoff between the demands for historical data and the capacity to store a large mass of data. This is similar to determining how long books stay in current publications' stacks before they are stored in the library archives. After the data have reached a specified maturity, they are moved to an archive. Since transaction level detail is of little value after the fact, the data in the warehouse are typically summarized. This also helps with storage issues. Summarizing should also resolve various issues of privacy and disclosure, resulting in the reduction of necessary access controls. Summarization places an additional requirement on the archiving process. The procedure used to summarize the data must also be time dated and stored. For example, "In 1991, the following departments were in the college of engineering...." needs to be available for those in 1998 who would restructure the college to have current program and departmental structure, reflecting the college's reorganization in 1994.

Only the elements from the operating systems that have lasting value for assessing the operations of the organization are summarized and archived. This is not a serious issue if one has been through the process of developing Administrative Database Master Files mentioned in the preceding chapter.

Time Variant. The data in a legacy system are accurate only at the time of extraction from the operating files. The data in a warehouse reflects a census date and does not change. If you count the number of students in the registrar's operating system on Monday, that same count on Tuesday will almost always be different. Because the census date database does not change, a count of the number of students will result in the same number regardless of when the count is taken, remaining conceptually correct until the next census date. The specific time of the census date is contained with warehouse elements. This is sometimes known as the time-date stamp and identifies the census date to the user. Data in a data warehouse are not updated, but rather another census extract is added to the warehouse on a predetermined schedule. The warehouse is simply a long series of data snapshots.

Data Flows

In developing the data warehouse, five types of data flows must be considered. Richard Hackathorn, (1995) described these flows in Data Warehousing Energizes Your Enterprise. The flows are related to the Information Support Circle illustrated in Figure 10.

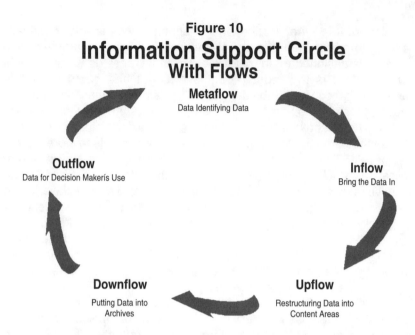

Figure 10
Information Support Circle
With Flows

Metaflow
Data Identifying Data

Outflow
Data for Decision Maker's Use

Inflow
Bring the Data In

Downflow
Putting Data into
Archives

Upflow
Restructuring Data into
Content Areas

The <u>Metaflow</u> (Identify Concepts and Measures) is the flow of data about the data. The <u>Inflow</u> (Collect and Store Data) of data brings the data to the warehouse from the operational systems. The <u>Upflow</u> (Restructure and Analyze Facts) of data combines and summarizes the detailed data and merges the various attributes around a subject-oriented structure. The <u>Downflow</u> (Deliver and Report Information) archives the elements, and the <u>Outflow</u> (Use and Influence Decisions) moves the data to the user. The quality of these flows depends on the quality of the steps taken to standardize the data and the codes described above. The quality of these flows also determines the value of the data to decision makers. Below are detailed explanations of these flows.

Metaflow. The process that moves meta-data in and through the warehouse to insure that data about data are available with the various flows is metaflow. Four activities are required to support metaflow. System modeling defines the structures and processes of the operational systems which are relevant to the warehouse. This should come as part of the code standardization process. Regulating is the process by which the appropriate person captures, validates, transforms, and relates key data to the relational form of the data structure. Synthesizing creates higher order data elements such as a data element defining "faculty" which is a flag derived from three- or four-data elements. Business modeling develops the rules of the organization's management, which can then be associated with the rules of the data warehouse to map the data architecture to the business architecture.

Inflow. Consolidating data from legacy systems is called inflow. It involves obtaining operational data, ensuring the standardization and cleaning processes were appropriate, adding fields to identify key group membership, and summarizing over unnecessary detail. Providing for this flow will produce data of some level of correctness, where the amount of effort spent cleaning the data is a management decision, balancing the level of correctness against the risks of using data which are less than perfect. Inflow can also include data brought in from external sources. For example, the average starting salary for faculty, from an external faculty survey, may be merged with the record of newly hired faculty at the institution. The inflow process will rapidly result in the identification of missing key variables and the lack of standardization.

Upflow. Combining, summarizing, and aggregating of data into subject areas in the warehouse is upflow. The data are rekeyed to critical variables, often the key variables identified in the standardization process. For example, facilities data may use the key of "building" in the warehouse while in the application system "room within building" is used. The upflow process summarizes data from all rooms which are in the same building. This process also involves pre-positioning data so subsets may be distributed to departmental warehouses. This includes restructuring the data into more accessible formats such as spreadsheets, graphical presentations, personal databases, and text documents

Downflow. The process of archiving the data is downflow. This results in more highly aggregated data being stored in a hierarchical archive, where it can be obtained for trend analyses and comparative studies. As noted earlier, there is a tradeoff in the amount of detail maintained and the amount of resources required by the archiving process. Similarly, it must be insured that the data warehouse is not populated with low-value data slowing performance and adding maintenance costs. As noted, it is good to store one more level of detail than is typically required by the decision makers and accompany the data with current cross-walk tables and time-date identification. The data element definitions must also be stored and custodial responsibility assigned. The need to control access to archived data is less stringent than it is for the operational systems since the data in the warehouse are "read" only and the summaries mask some of the detail. However, the issues of data sensitivity do not completely disappear.

Outflow. The process where data becomes available to the customer is outflow. The two activities at this step are accessing and delivering. The components of the delivery function also include some of the capability which support reporting where the delivered data are interfaced with information about specific situations. Reporting requirements can range from simple ad hoc queries to frequently requested formats and tables at the same level of detail as in the warehouse. The warehouse needs to be integrated with common access tools which are consistent with the ability and the need of the decision makers. The more progressive tools should also provide the ability to pinpoint the distribution of data extracts and summaries to specific users. This is a boundary step of empowering end users to be cooperators of a data warehouse function.

Involving Others in the Organization

The process of managing data and the coordination of data processing functions require the involvement of numerous individuals. These individuals will often not be close working colleagues. Forming various groups to focus on data management issues will help leverage the contribution each can make.

Data Stewards Group. These are the individuals who deal with data in standard operational bases. They need to identify current problems which exist in maintaining the integrity of the data. Information is shared about best practices for standardizing, documenting, and sharing information. They should propose standards for their local data elements and develop the requirements for data management tools, techniques, and procedures such as the data dictionary, data validation, data correction, and data integration. Finally, they should apply and test standards, tools, techniques, and procedures as they evolve and then make recommendations for changes as appropriate.

Administrators Group. These are the senior administrators who have the authority to make decisions across the various operational databases. They need to consider the problems they recognize in the delivery and use of data. They also address questions of conflicts such as, who is the custodian, what is the source of certain data elements, and who is responsible for official codes. They need to assist with the coordination of standardization activities across departments and system areas.

Information Systems Group. These are the managers of the information technology. This group should also include some of the major users and custodians. Here, individuals can investigate, refine, and develop automated data management tools and techniques such as the data dictionary, edit and validation routines, integrity audits, relational systems for decision support, and readily accessible use documentation. It should also investigate and recommend appropriate platforms and strategies for distributing decision support information to university administrators and executives.

Management Group. This is a group of midlevel managers who are responsible for the day-to-day management of the organization, and who depend on the integrity of data. This group deals with access, timing, integrity checking, and other issues which impact the value of the data. These people set the objectives and tactics of the data management initiative on an annual basis. The group also identifies the planning needs for data. It reviews project plans and progress reports. These managers review recommendations and products, and endorse action or adoption of standard procedures. Depending on the culture and courage of the institution, this group may even be authorized to make policy and define procedures.

Decision Support Group. This is a smaller group which takes the recommendations of the management group and discusses strategy for implementation. It may be an office of an organizational unit the institution has designated to support the management of the data. In instances when the institution is not willing to make the commitment to coordinate the management of the data centrally, it may be made up of representatives from three or four key areas who meet periodically to review progress in their areas.

Operational System User Group. This group of individuals focuses on the use of a specific system. For example, there might be a student data users group. This group can vary in formality with functions ranging from authorizing code changes to sharing effective ways to develop reports using the data. Where there are users who have dependence across systems, forming a cross-functional group of administrative systems users may be beneficial.

Implementing the Broker Role

The data warehouse, discussed above, is the blending together of multiple tools with multiple needs of managers and coordinating related data management activities across the operational breath of the institution. This typically is not one of those "build it and they will come" endeavors. However, the numerous tradeoffs such as detail and capacity balanced against speed and expense are not simple to resolve. There are no easy answers. Mature negotiation and the bargaining skill of the broker, along with help from key managers and administrators, are required for selecting appropriate levels of aggregation, time-frame data maintenance in the active warehouse, involvement of managers, subject nature of the data structure, and policies requiring the proper processing of data. To accomplish this, an individual at the institution should be assigned the responsibilities identified in Table 3.

Table 3

BROKER RESPONSIBILITIES
Clarify needs: identify decisions and determine involvement of the administrative information infrastructure for administrative, academic, and external users; determine mutual needs for data and the associated timing of uses
Document means: develop and disseminate means for obtaining, retaining, maintaining, explaining, analyzing, and exchanging information; use feasible technology; involve users; visit someone who has what you want
Define content: coordinate development and refinement of various management data policies and procedures; relate to other operational processes; associate compliance with expectations and rewards
Develop data: direct projects to enhance management data and administrative information support; check with users, look for bottleneck problems and root-cause problems; prototype improvement and demonstrate results
Implement use: teach various users the skills to use institutional and external data; share alternative data sets; provide one-stop shopping for monitoring institutional success factors

Implementing broker responsibilities will most likely change the way in which the institutional research function operates. In Table 4, specific duties are enumerated which will result in the implementation of the broker responsibilities.

Brokers need to have technical ability, managerial skills, and knowledge about the specific institution at which they are working. They will need to work closely with those in information resource management/information systems units, where the technical work to build the data warehouse and bridge it to legacy systems is typically done. This is not a place to learn on the job because of the heavy interaction with key administrators who have their own concerns. Further, those who support the development of the data warehouse must have a strong interest in continued scholarly growth to deal with the rapid development in the area.

The broker function must be the opportunistic application of organization vision to operational resource realities. The function depends greatly on the ability and willingness of the custodians to create data as an asset to the institution. Success depends on the central coordination of the data resource and the availability of some type of data warehouse. In addition

Table 4

BROKER DUTIES
Support the continued improvement of the office ability to provide high quality service to its various customers
Maintain a high level of professional knowledge in hardware, software, and organizational processes related to the management of data using information resources
Analyze institutional needs for improved data and information and integrating those needs with other projects
Integrate the needs of administrative and managerial users with the availability of data and the capability of technology to produce improved data support
Develop conceptual management models and define components of management data and administrative information
Manage various projects and technical work groups of professional faculty and staff
Learn, use, and teach various methodologies to improve the administrative process based on the availability of data
Develop and implement training programs for institutional personnel on the concepts and capabilities of hardware and software related to management data and administrative information
Pursue personal professional and scholarly development including participation in a network of professionals at comparable institutions and serve in professional associations
Represent the office and, where appropriate, the institution at various system, state, and national activities, negotiations, and presentations (NCES, ACE, NASLGCU, AIR, AACC, etc.)

to the warehouse, there needs to be extract tools, data handling tools, and relational database management systems.

Making the Broker Job a Success

Above, we have outlined specific tasks that are expected to be performed by the Broker. Success in these tasks will require the development of an understanding of the decision making cycle at the institution and the relationship between key people and the decisions they make. Facilitate the focus of research questions by grouping customers with projects to take advantage of common issues and common responsibilities and common needs. Meet and involve subject matter experts (faculty) in areas of concern. Learn from them the biases of their assumptions and methodologies when problem solving. Continue professional development, by joining AIR, and/or other professional organizations that can contribute to personal competency. Finally, maintain an ethical and fair balance. Where a professional stands should be a function of where a professional sits, and this is respected.

The next step is to look at the integration of information into the institution's knowledge base. Users are managers who are interested in the flow of facts and the integration of facts with existing knowledge. This process, which extends knowledge and forms new intelligence around decision points, is discussed in the next chapter.

CHAPTER 6
THE MANAGER—REALIZING VALUE FROM DATA

We need understanding businesses devoted to making information accessible and comprehensible; we need new ways of interpreting the data that increasingly directs our lives and new models for making it usable and understandable, for transforming it into information. We need to re-educate the people who generate information to improve its performance, and we, as consumers, must become more adroit as receivers if we are ever to recover from information anxiety. (Wurman, p. 50)

The manager is the person who receives information from the broker. He or she uses it to describe a situation, select and evaluate alternatives, make a decision, or defend and advocate previous decisions. Managers' actions integrate information into the institution's knowledge base, thereby reducing uncertainty and increasing "organizational intelligence." Usually, the manager deals with uncertainty and makes decisions with less than perfect information.

What Does a Manager Do?

Managers must monitor and measure the value of information they receive and judiciously use it to add value to their existing knowledge base. The problems they solve must be important to the institution. As such, managers are in the best position to identify changes in business rules that must be reflected by the organization's data. They need to educate the supplier, or the data custodian, about the needs for data, and how the data are used. The custodian can then capture and store the most appropriate data. The manager must also know about the different types of tools, and technologies that can be used to access data. Whether an individual or several individuals establish the link between the data and the tools, it is critical that it be established. To accomplish these tasks, there are a number of specific responsibilities that must be accepted by the manager. These responsibilities are listed in Table 5.

In order to successfully meet these responsibilities, the manager must recognize threats to internal, external, and construct validity. These characteristics of quality decision-support data and information are critical. Data processes and analyses must be continuously monitored and tweaked to reflect the institution's business rules in line with validity concerns.

Internal Validity. The sufficiency, relevancy, accuracy, reliability, and timeliness of the data define the internal validity of the data. The manager must know how to evaluate the information provided in terms of sufficiency

Table 5

MANAGER RESPONSIBILITIES
The manager must ensure that the organization serves its basic purpose of producing specific goods or services. This implies that the manager understands the institution's purpose and can determine whether the organization is moving in that direction.
The manager should create and sustain a level of organizational stability which will be manageable. Excessive instability prevents effectiveness.
The manager aligns strategic purposes with the resources of the organization. With a sense of the mission, the environment, the threats, the opportunities, and the alternatives, the manager needs to provide direction for the organization and focus change in a feasible way.
The manager makes sure that the needs of the key stakeholders in the organization are met. For many of us, this is the state legislature, taxpayers, students who pay the bills, faculty who determine governance issues, or some combination of these key influences. The key is to understand the interest of these diverse groups and integrate their concerns into a coherent strategy.
The manager serves as the strategic informational link between the organization and its external constituents. As that link, the manager must defend the organization, advocate its positions, articulate its needs for resources, monitor external issues, and disseminate information to internal constituents. The flow of information is characterized as "continuous, real-time, and specific in its detail" and not as "long-term" or "big picture."
The manager works within the formal authority system of the organization. The manager must delegate, appoint, and anoint the people responsible, and held accountable, for organizational activities.

and relevancy, so that only the amount of information needed for the specific situation is brought forward. He or she must also evaluate the information's accuracy and reliability so that confidence in the information's quality or usefulness can be evaluated. Finally, timeliness in bringing the information forward is critical in order that it is converted into intelligence before decisions are made and actions taken.

External Validity. The degree to which data and information can be appropriately applied to a specific situation is external validity. The manager must have the skills to interpret and effectively use information to assure the external validity of the information. If the information is not relevant to the situation, then all analyses, interpretations, etc. will not be relevant. Since the specific situation, as well as the elements of the decision, is known only to the manager, or user of the information, it is clear that the manager must carry this responsibility.

Construct Validity. Managers are responsible for monitoring and measuring the value of the information. They must integrate the information into the existing set of knowledge, information, and data about issues. This process must add value to the previous set of relevant knowledge. The problems solved must be important to the institution. This is often referred to as the construct validity of the information and represents consideration of the degree to which "as is" becomes "to be." This step typically triggers a change in the manager's beliefs, creating uncertainties, which, in turn, generate the need for new decisions, and the cycle of information support is repeated.

Systems and Tools for Managers

The information the manager needs comes from different support systems, depending upon the need. These systems range from transaction processing in operational systems to sophisticated expert systems.

The Operational System. These data systems are the applications systems that support a particular function, such as accounting, payroll, etc. They are also often referred to as OLTP systems (Online Transaction Processing). They are designed to optimize online data entry and the processing of large numbers of transactions. These systems support institutional operations such as payroll and student registration. The data change rapidly, and continually, always reflecting the most recent status of any given data element. OLTP systems provide answers to such questions as: What happened last? or What is John Doe's benefit status? The basic architecture of this system supports online updating, and rapid response to queries usually focusing on a particular transactional unit of information. A classic example of an OLTP system outside of higher education is an airline reservation system.

Management Information Systems. The system architecture that most readily supports management information is the data warehouse. Data is captured from the various operational systems, converted, (cleaned up and standardized) aggregated, and summarized. The data warehouse contains historical data, in both detail and summary form. It is a collection of dated snapshots of data designed to support management decisions.

The data, once loaded, is not updated. The data from the warehouse are used to answer questions such as: How has graduate student enrollment changed over the past 10 years? and How does the percentage of minorities in all departments, and colleges, in 1985 compare with that in 1995? The architecture of this system supports functions such as trend analyses. It is designed to support queries that access large amounts of information.

Performance Analysis Systems. These systems include decision support and executive information systems. They support many different types of analyses: trend analysis, what if, etc. "What revenue will be generated by increasing the out-of-state enrollment?" is the type of question investigated using performance analysis systems. The data warehouse provides the data that can then be further analyzed with performance analysis systems. Another term for many of these systems is Online Analytical Processing systems or OLAP. The architecture for many of these systems is a multidimensional cube, set of cubes, or arrays. The ways the user wants to view the data (the dimensions) are defined, along with the elements the user wants to aggregate (the measures). The tools then build a model and create a structure that supports rapid access of the predefined data elements. With most of the products currently available, the data is aggregated and loaded into a multidimensional cube. The cube architecture ensures rapid response. When the dimensions and measures are appropriately defined and packaged, the manager, or user, can perform analyses that range from basic statistical analyses, such as max, min, mean, and ranges to more complex analyses such as linear regression. The complexity of the analysis is dependent upon the capability of the OLAP product. All of these products allow the user to "explore" the data, and display the results in many different graphical views. The architecture of this system provides rapid access to information through a very user-friendly interface.

Tools for Information Access

There are several different types of tools that the manager can use to access data. They include:

Desktop Database Management Systems. With the use of a desktop DBMS and the ability to retrieve selected data in a standard database format, the manager will have maximum flexibility for manipulating data, migrating data to other desktop products, and producing reports.

Spreadsheets. Spreadsheets can be used to do data analysis and some reporting. They can even be used to create databases.

Word Processors. Reports and documentation can be accessed and viewed with word processors.

Web Browsers. The World Wide Web potentially provides an excellent platform for accessing meta-data, packaged data subsets, reports, etc. The web provides platform independent access. This is an area that is just beginning to develop in terms of its potential for decision support. Many organizations are implementing "intranets" to provide their managers with both internal and external data and information.

OLAP Products. These products provide rapid access to data with Graphical User Interface (GUI). They provide standard analysis functions, and support drill-down/drill-up processes, point and click, drag and drop navigation, and exception highlighting. They complement the data warehouse.

Desktop Statistical Products. There are several desktop statistical products for providing analysis. Probably the best known products are SAS, Minitab, and SPSS. There are also special purpose programs and programming languages for more complex needs.

Ad hoc Query and Data Browsers. There are several easy to use products which provide users with access to data in relational databases. They support ad hoc query, so the user can construct and execute a simple request using an English-like language. Most of these will provide the user with a formatted report or the option to save data in a format which can be used by a spreadsheet, a desktop database, or a desktop word processor. These tools greatly enhance the utility of the data warehouse.

Institutional Research Support for the Manager Role

> *The information-transmitting function is crucial to organizational decision making, for it almost always involves acts of selection or 'filtering' by the information source...Hence, the subordinate acts as an information filter and in this way secures a large influence over the decisions the superior can and does reach. (Simon, p. 284)*

The manager is the nerve center of the organization. He or she continually seeks and receives information from numerous sources and must reconcile the information with organizational needs. The manager uses the data to test the validity of a perception against the reality of the situation. The manager detects changes, identifies problems and opportunities, understands the options, makes decisions, and provides key stakeholders with an understanding of both the problem, and the solution (Mintzberg, 1973). The manager's performance depends upon proper analyses, which will restructure and summarize data into the most usable form. Institutional research often functions as an integrator and transmitter of the data.

While institutional researchers do not typically see themselves as filters and integrators, these may well be their most influential role. The typical institutional research mission is to enhance institutional effectiveness by providing information which supports and strengthens operations management, decision making, and planning processes of the executive administration. These activities include:

1. Performing studies that describe, analyze, and interpret the policies, functions and activities of the institution for the executive-level management (the President, the Provost, the Executive Vice President, etc.)

2. Supporting the development of management information capabilities throughout the institution.

3. Providing consistent and reliable statistical summaries of selected university-wide data and coordinating IPEDS and similar external reporting for the college or university.

4. Supporting the standardization of institutional administrative data codes and documentation.

5. Providing a credible ethical source of information. Making all data and information available within the constraints of confidentiality, remaining sensitive to the gray area between slanting data, and supporting the institution's decisions.

6. Training users in basic data collection and data analysis skills.

The services implied in this mission focus on bringing together data, integrating much of them with qualitative factors, reducing the complexity of the facts, and bringing them to the attention of the manager. The skill-set needed to provide the services (listed below) is an obvious demonstration of the institutional researcher's interest in all aspects of institutional data management.

- **Problem Identification** involves identifying problem areas where decisions need to be made, searching for the broadest range of situations, and considering alternatives and their feasibility. Alternatives might include forecasting studies, market research studies, and anticipating gaps in strategies.

- **Cost-Benefit Analysis** involves the detailed consideration of the resources required for specific strategies and evaluation of these resources in light of the outcomes from these strategies. Outcomes assessment is an example of cost-benefit analyses.

64

- **Model Building** is the process of simulating complex events with either simulation or mathematical equations which, when taken together, will anticipate an outcome caused by a complex set of events.

- **Contingency Planning** comes from developing strategies for dealing with undesirable events and is designed to reduce the negative impact of those undesirable events.

- **Real-time Analysis** is the use of an analytical methodology "on-the-fly" to look at the desirability of alternatives, as they become apparent.

- **Project Monitoring** is using resource flows, monitoring activities, and comparative analyses to help keep a project on time and on target.

- **Adaptive Planning** is the process of building plans which can be modified to anticipate and profit from changing issues in a dynamic situation. These plans have multiple strategies and build multiple accomplishments into a tactic (Mintzberg, 1973).

While this list above is not exhaustive, it does demonstrate that information needs require the ability to use basic analytical tools in more complex combinations, especially when the emphasis is on the context and the use of the results.

Supporting the Manager Role

The data must be used in order to have value in the organization. The function of use and influence is different from the other functions in the Information Support Circle in that executing this function is mostly beyond the control of the person involved with the management of the data. The role of the integrator becomes one of exercising indirect influence. This requires understanding barriers and unobtrusively attempting to overcome each barrier.

The barriers experienced in the use and influence of the data typically include a lack of interest from senior administrators and a lack of cooperation from contacts in offices supplying the data, the lack of consistent formats, and the possible sensitivity of the data, particularly if trends are moving in an embarrassing direction. How can the institutional research function help overcome these barriers?

Influence can be greatly increased by institutional awareness of the organization, its culture, and its context. This does not come from the facts or their direct use in a situation, but rather from the means by which situations are chosen and restructured to increase knowledge. Institutional research can cultivate knowledge by helping users place the facts into an organizational context, i.e., the institution's culture, values, and goals.

Some examples of institutional research activities, which can increase the influence of facts through the contextual knowledge of their use, include:

- Increasing the visibility of the use of the data and information through the use of examples

- Demonstrating the professional virtue of the information source by being credible, demonstrating integrity, and remaining silent until appropriate

- Obtaining the strategic support of those who can use the results

- Focusing the results of research on professional commitments and concerns of powerful individuals

- Leveraging mutual support and concerns of various groups by looking for conceptual models which provide an overlap of concerns—in other words, form coalitions around the information

- Strengthening functional authority by training others

- Influencing the management of data and information through the ability to work with the data and tools, applying these skills appropriately to specific situations

- Coordinating data, computers, and individuals interested in the results

- Using the technical tools available to access and analyze the data

- Providing credibility through secure, accurate, and stable information

- Using techniques to reduce great volumes of data into a structure which can be digested by the decision maker

- Providing insight about the data and the decision process

- Generalizing the results into a use, which is sufficient to cover the problem and is for the most part related to the problem or issue at hand

- Suggesting specific measures to consider

Other proactive strategies for overcoming barriers include:

- Creating user interest in improving their skills through training, enabling them to do more of their own research

• Limiting information to the key issues in the situation

• Having information available just before it is needed

While institutional research functions and offices typically possess considerable technical skills and are usually eager to extend these skills, their mission, skill-sets and expertise typically revolve around research and analytical processing. The use of internal administrative data for trend, comparative, and predictive analyses, and reporting depends on a standardized support environment where regularly scheduled data extracts are taken from principal transactional databases, integrated as a "warehouse" of data and with external data where appropriate. These data are accessed with software that supports merging, retrieval, analysis, interpretation, and reporting functions. From department-to-department, criteria can be modified to meet specific needs of users.

As data and analysis tools are more widely available to a variety of internal and external users, institutional research functions will continue to evolve both as a major user of administrative systems data and as an information broker, providing integrated data and training in analytical processing to users. The speed of this evolution and the quality of support will depend on the value of the data. This, in turn, depends, not only on the commitment of the institution to support organizational changes necessary for data management, but also depends upon the quality of the technical resources available for its data management.

Making the Manager Job a Success

To accomplish the tasks outlined above, we offer the following as a foundation for success. Read The Fifth Discipline and other books about the learning organization. Avoid gimmicks or books with "minute" or "secrets" in the title. Get out and meet people who are important to the successful operation of the data management process. This includes senior administrators as well as those doing the work. Develop a vision of where the organization is going, what needs to be done to get there, what the limits are for feasible solutions, when decisions have to be made, and what problems seem to exist. Begin studies, group projects, and tasks to identify what information is needed, within what time frames and at what cost. Finally, visit other managers who are successful, and share what is found by joining professional organizations of such managers in areas as SCUP, NACUBO, ACRO, etc.

67

CHAPTER 7
GETTING STARTED: JUST DO IT

An Irish Prayer

May those who love us, love us,
And those that don't love us,
May God turn their hearts.

And if He doesn't turn their hearts,
May he turn their ankles,
So we'll know them by their limp.

(AIR Newsletter, Sept. 14, 1992, Original source lost in antiquity)

Colleges and universities are complex adaptive systems. They consist of departments, offices, and managers who should be continually striving to adapt to a rapidly changing and uncertain environment. These managers and their staffs need data and information to reduce uncertainty. This helps them to explore, clarify, and define strategies and tactics. Complex adaptive systems will be successful if there are large numbers of individuals with a similar purpose, with usable mechanisms for learning, and a source of energy to create activity.

In the preceding chapters, the management of quality data and information is defined as a complex process. The data custodian, the broker, and the manager need to work together to transform data into information, and use that information or organizational intelligence to define and solve current problems and anticipate future challenges.

Managing Data for Information

Learning about the management of data requires more than a set of technical skills and abilities. Management of data requires an understanding of the organizational processes of the institution, and an understanding of the environment in which the data are both produced and used. Dealing with this complexity and establishing value-added niches requires an understanding of the general organizational process of adaptation. What are the basic strategies and tactics required to change the organization? What are the issues involved in the change, and what are the lessons we have learned from working to change and improve the management of data?

Properties of Successful Information Support

Two key characteristics or properties were discussed in Chapter 2, which are necessary for the successful transformation of data into useful information and increased organizational intelligence. These properties are dependency and cooperation. Here, we develop the discussion of these properties in the context of the Information Support Circle.

Dependency

As we have seen, each function in the Information Support Circle (Figure 2) is dependent upon the previous function. This dependency provides the basis for focusing our efforts on the best strategy for increasing the value of data to the institution. The quality of each function is limited by the quality of the preceding function. The foundation for this premise is basic measurement theory. If a measure has no reliability, it can have no validity. The value of using the results of measurement (e.g., information) is limited by the ability to replicate results. Nonetheless, the functions of the Information Support Circle have limitations, which are discussed below.

- The ability to identify the problem and measure the proper factors (content validity) is limited by the ability to deal with the problems in a systematic and relevant fashion (Use and Influence Decisions).

- The value from collecting and storing a valuable data asset (reliability) is limited by a lack of understanding of the importance of the various issues (Identify Concepts and Measures).

- The value obtained from restructuring and analyzing the data is to understand what is happening (internal validity) and is limited by an ability to obtain data which is consistent and stable (Collect and Store Data).

- The value of information delivered and included in reporting to generalize the results (external validity) is limited by the ability to interpret what was done in the analysis and by the understanding of causality (Restructure and Analyze Facts).

- The value from the use of the information to influence the situation (construct validity) is limited by the ability to generalize the information to the situation of concern (Deliver and Report Information).

The key to improvement is the ability to recognize and learn from these limitations. If the quality of a function in the Information Support Circle is limited by the quality of the preceding function, then the only way to improve that function is by improving the preceding function. Improvement for the entire support process is limited by the quality of the weakest function (the weakest link). This conclusion is consistent with the conclusions of those who look at root-cause analysis. Correcting problems, which are not the root cause, will not produce major improvement. Improving the analysis of the data will not overcome the lack of reliable data. Improving the quality of data will not increase the value of information support, if the decision makers do not properly identify measures that reflect the issues. Developing standardized data when the lack of standardization is the root problem, however, will improve the value of all other functions.

Cooperation

Cooperation among the manager, the broker, and the data custodian is critically important. The vision of the executive needs to be shared with the entire organization. Data custodians must share the experiences they have working with the institutional activities, and the measurement of those activities. The brokers must work with both groups to analyze and restructure the data. Instilling and encouraging cooperation may be the most challenging aspect of improving data management. It requires someone, a champion, who will motivate, and facilitate conflict resolution. It further requires a shared commitment to the institution's vision, a sense of how the institution needs to change. Finally, it requires an understanding of the way people react to change. Cooperation can overcome the problematic situation that results when the manager makes a request of the broker who in turn makes a request of the custodian. The custodian collects the data, gives them to the broker, who then analyzes them and shares the results with the manager. Very often each of the players in this chain of events becomes frustrated as they attempt to respond in a vacuum without the benefit of systematic thinking or the culture of cooperation. On the other hand, if players are cooperating, there is one central conversation rather than four linear conversations, and work can potentially be done in parallel, rather than sequentially, leading to faster and better solutions to problems.

Managing Change Processes: Basic Models

It has been said, "nothing changes if nothing changes." Improvement requires change and change requires effort. In order to sustain and nurture a change effort, you must have a personal understanding of the change process, and the impact it has upon others. Following are three models for understanding the way change occurs and the way people react to change. These three models relate, in sequence, to activities performed by individuals working in groups. Of course, there are many other models, and as you work with change, you may develop your own. As illustrated in Figure 11, the three change models come together at certain points as change occurs across the campus.

The first model frames the change process for activities in terms of the Plan-Do-Check-Act continuous improvement cycle. During the Plan stage, we collect viewpoints, and based upon these viewpoints, determine

Figure 11
Change Processes

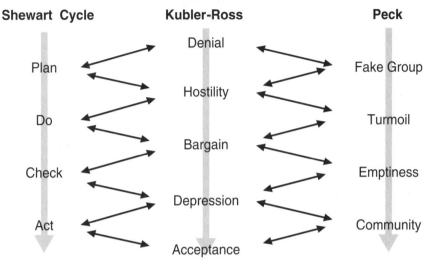

Shewart Cycle	Kubler-Ross	Peck

problem areas, scope, possible causes, and alternative solutions. During the Do stage, prototyped solutions are developed, and the results measured. This is the stage where change begins to occur. In the Check stage, the results of the prototype are evaluated in respect to anticipated results, or against a baseline, to determine the impact of the change. In the Act stage, the change is integrated into organizational processes, and the improvement change cycle begins again.

The second model is the response of individuals to change, illustrated by the Kubler-Ross sequence for grieving, i.e. denial, hostility, bargaining, depression, and acceptance. It recognizes that change is first and foremost, the loss of the way "we have always done it" and this loss is always traumatic, as comfort zones are threatened. As the Plan emerges, there is disbelief (denial) that a problem exists. During the next phase, the Do stage, there is a reaction to the change (hostility). During the Check stage, invariably bargaining is attempted. There is the stated desire by those involved to make the best possible change, which too often turns out to be the least amount of change. When finally there is a realization that real change is inevitable, people are often overwhelmed (depressed). As they begin to learn the new process, and, particularly, if they have some influence, depression is replaced with acceptance, during the Act stage. As improvement becomes obvious, individuals not only accept the change but also take personal pride in improvement.

The third model provides an understanding of group response to change. F. Scott Peck, in The Different Drummer - Community Making and

<u>Peace</u>, discusses four stages that a group goes through before it operates as a team, with a commitment to improvement or a true "community." These stages are pseudo-community, chaos, emptiness, and, finally, community. During the development of a new central mission or purpose, the group will first act as though it is already working together, operating as a true team. This is pseudo-community or false community. The group is not working together, but feels it can avoid change if it "gets along" and avoids differences, conflicts, and confrontations.

Since conflict is inevitable, the group will eventually move into the chaotic phase. Conflict surfaces as individuals experience and express hostility toward those members proposing new and different ways of doing things. There will be well-intentioned attempts to obliterate differences by offering simple cures, and bargaining will ensue. During the third phase, the group admits there are new options, and they experience emptiness as they begin to let go of the old and seek out the new. Feelings of depression accompany the realization that change is required. In the final phase, the individuals become a true functioning group or community with an acceptance of new ways of doing things. They, the group and individually, gain energy from the shared experience of confronting issues and finding solutions.

These change models are not principles of individual or group behavior, but do seem to reflect the way many of us respond to change. They are important to consider, since they clearly indicate that change and improvement are difficult, and that significant amounts of resolve and patience are needed to undergo real change and thereby improve.

We can speed the naturally occurring stages in the change process by employing five strategies (Geller, 1989) that will ease the impact:

Awareness and Education. People must be given sound reasons for change. This will improve the acceptance of change. Awareness and education seems to best occur in small groups and include interactive demonstrations and discussions.

Verbal and Written Messages. Messages can be effective. There are appropriate times to use verbal messages and appropriate times to use written messages. Both types of communication must be concise and easy to understand.

Modeling and Demonstrations. Modeling is a way of prototyping a process or change and documenting the anticipated results. It can help people think through the process and anticipate outcomes.

Commitment and Goal Setting. Individuals must participate in goal setting. If the goal setting process is accomplished with both individual and group participation, it can enhance commitment to the goals and buy-in by individuals to the process.

Engineering and Design Strategies. An organization must be structured to support change. It is critical that procedures and policies make the change easier. The reporting structure (management structure) of the organization can also either facilitate or impede change. The structure, policies, etc., that will support change ideally will be in place before you begin as structure must follow strategy.

The Culture of Change

There are several cultural indicators we should observe during transition that can alert us to areas that might require particular attention. These indicators can also help us assess whether we have truly evolved to a "change and improve" culture, or case-in-point, to a new data management culture.

- Do people openly acknowledge and value working relationships with individuals across the organization?

- Do people claim ownership for problems as opposed to blaming others or the system?

- Do people accept working with others at levels above and below them within the organization's hierarchy?

- Are people willing to take risks and embark on new ventures?

- Are people receptive to others, seeking input, and considering a variety of perspectives?

- Do people who represent different interest groups make an effort to make contact and communicate with each other?

To the extent that we can answer "yes" to each of these questions, we are well-positioned to evolve a data management culture that indeed embraces "new ideas for new challenges." We must remember that change is a process and that changes in attitude, however subtle, signal progress. These include shifts from managing to leading, from control to coaching, from quantity to quality, from opinion to information, from resistant to change to open to change, from people as commodities to people as resources, from suspicion to trust, from compliance to commitment, from internal focus to customer focus, from individual to team, and from detection to prevention (Plice, 1992). All of these transitions are part of growing a data management culture. It is important to watch for these transitions and recognize them as gains in terms of awareness and commitment. They signal emerging pockets of support. Data management can no longer be regarded as a technical issue. There will need to be changes in our organizations. Matrix

73

organizations and cross-functional teams focused on specific tasks or problems must become commonplace. This places the data users and those who need information in direct contact with the data suppliers. Those who produce data and information for decision making must shift from the data analyst role to the role of facilitator and broker.

The organization which tries to distribute information without management processes to define and document data will fail. The organization which does not push out the data and transform it into information will fall behind more progressive competitors. The organization which does not restructure to support a revised decision structure will frustrate its employees who will, in turn, waste valuable time and energy on feudal turf battles. The organization, which does not continually train its employees to manage and use information, will make questionable decisions.

We must step forward and nurture a data management culture. Deal and Kennedy suggest we must resist the temptation to roll up our sleeves and wade directly into the resolution of the problem as traditional managers if we truly want to encourage lasting change or transformation to a new culture. They suggest as an alternative the notion of a "symbolic manager" who recognizes that the solution is to rely on individuals in the culture to meander their way to a solution.

"New ideas for new challenges" amounts to creating a web of intelligence from the ideas and vision we have today. The web of intelligence is the new data management culture. It must be anchored by educated, empowered people who perform relevant and timely activities using sophisticated navigational and analytical tools on properly integrated quality data from both internal and external sources.

Strategies and Tactics

The ultimate measure of success for creating a management information infrastructure is the extent data are used in decision making. It is only when executives begin to reference data/information in decision making that the best intelligence will be applied to the challenges they face. There are several strategies and tactics that can be used to help those who have been inspired by this book to create and establish a management information infrastructure. It is absolutely critical that the linkage between the data and the need for information is established. Below are some specific steps you can take to establish this linkage in your own organization.

- Market the value of the information, and the benefits of having information in order to understand issues. The entire process of creating a data management culture and management information infrastructure is extremely complicated, and it is very easy for people to loose sight of the tangible benefits. Throughout the process, you must present the need in terms that managers can understand.

- Identify areas where quality data are critically needed and are especially inadequate. One of these areas may be an appropriate area to prototype. Picking a visible area to prototype will help demonstrate the potential of the project and also gain support for the project.

- Obtain and train the best people to work on the information. The project requires many different skills. Train people in project management, processes, and technology.

- Attract resource support by helping to diagnose problems. This relates to developing a prototype. If you can solve a problem for someone, they will be likely to help you obtain the resource support you need.

- Adjust the ends to fit the means. With an undertaking that is this complex, it is easy to overreach. Make sure you keep the end in sight. Then break the project into manageable phases and celebrate iterative successes. This will help sustain the interest and motivation of all concerned.

- Do not set impossible goals. Again, with an undertaking as large as this, it is easy to define goals that are not reasonable. This undermines the entire project, and is a way to ensure failure. Set achievable goals and identify reachable milestones. Measure and communicate the progress you make. When possible, identify multiple strategies to achieve your goals.

- Define and redefine plans and progress. This requires breaking the project into phases. Define the first phase as your stage-setting accomplishments, the current phase in detail, and third phase in concept. When you complete a phase, define the next one in detail, adjusting to include what you have learned, and what you can do to improve. Never lose sight of the overall information infrastructure you are striving to create.

Lessons Learned

The organizations that will truly excel in the future will be the organizations that discover how to tap people's commitment and capacity to learn at all levels of the organization. (Senge quoted in Merlyn, p. 40)

As you move your institution into more systematic data management, you become increasingly aware of the people processes that influence the success of what you do and the types of issues you face. There is no guarantee that the issues you face will be the same as those which others have faced, but we believe that lessons our colleagues and we have learned can be shared with positive effects. It is in that spirit that the following are shared.

- Some non-performers will begin to perform as they are motivated by recognition of their unique expertise, opportunities to take on different tasks in the more fluid organization, and challenged to think creatively and take risks.

- Those unwilling or unable to deal with change may leave or relocate within the organization when their worn rhetoric and claims that "this is the way we have always done it" are challenged and/or ignored.

- New leaders will emerge from those who are flexible, those who are committed and determined, those who nurture growth and learning, and those who communicate a vision for the future.

- Roles will swap with some non-technicians moving into more technical endeavors and some technicians taking on managerial responsibilities.

- Understanding that all change is a step-by-step process can ease the trauma. When we clarify where we are in relation to where we have been and where we are going, we are less fearful and, therefore, willing to step out of the comfort zone of the familiar and participate in transformation.

- Training is essential to survive. People want to work smarter and deliver a valued product. To do this, they need to constantly upgrade their skill-set. This happens only when someone in the organization understands that the future of the organization rests with people, not technological tools, and is, therefore, willing to invest accordingly.

- The institutional research function must be involved in a complement of training, covering everything from new technology tools, project management, and working in teams, to the way the mission and purpose of the institution is changing. Knowledge builds confidence and confident people will step out, deal with change, and work for continuous improvement.

- It is important to have a recognized organizational function directly involved with managing the distribution of data to the users. Someone should feel that his or her salary is directly based on the success of the data management strategy. This function must coordinate data management at all levels of the organization and assist users with the resulting products. It may also be responsible for the more traditional data administration functions of custodian support, standards administration, and information systems planning. Another strategy is to provide a technical support bridge between users and the computer technology function.

- The new organization should not become involved in managing technology. It should remain attentive to managing data and information and, as such, may logically affiliate with any one of several existing central university functions depending largely on where users currently seek and find answers to their information requests.

- The enemy of continual gradual improvement is burnout. To avoid burnout, celebrate incremental victories. It is also helpful if workgroups initiate communication about expectations and personal goals and then work toward mutually beneficial outcomes. Always take time to assess progress and help others understand that every improvement is a success.

In Conclusion

As stated in the Foreword, this monograph represents a work-in-progress. Technology is constantly changing and making new things possible. Meanwhile, the rightsizing/downsizing or simply restructuring organizational structures, processes, and resources places additional pressures on those trying to lead change. Perhaps the greatest unmet challenges rest in the measurement and communication of our progress in ways that facilitate the integration of judgment and intelligence. While we have changed and grown, we know there is much more change and growth ahead. Our choices are limited: lead, follow, or get out of the way!

 **SUCCESS**

- **Increase visibility and use of information**
- **Be credible**
- **Obtain strategic support**
- **Leverage mutual concerns of various groups**
- **Train others**

APPENDIX

Information Support Audit

The improvement of the information support will be best accomplished by starting with a realistic idea of how well the existing process supports the needs of your institution or organization. In order to assist in this evaluation, we have prepared a set of 100 items, which look at the quality of the various functions involved in supporting information.

For each item, consider if it represents the situation with which you are familiar. If so, circle the item number. At the end of the set of items, add up the number of circled items. The best place for your efforts are with the function in which the lowest number of items is circled.

Identify Concepts and Measures

1. A clear understanding of explicitly stated purposes and goals for various major programs and units exists across the institution.

2. A flow chart of the relationship of various data systems (and information) and decisions has been developed (as in Information Architecture).

3. Individuals are given responsibilities and authorities for specific objectives.

4. Executives welcome questions about strategic issues and key stakeholders.

5. Technicians and analysts are involved in goal setting at all levels of the institution.

6. Everyone understands the management processes used in the institution and the institutional research office.

7. There is consensus about what variables are important to describe specific situations and events.

8. Important (if not all) issues are measured with objective facts.

9. Believable and accepted models have been developed to explain anticipated outcomes.

10. Most user questions can be answered from census-date databases or an institutional fact book.

11. Standard definitions exist across the institution for key concepts such as faculty, student, and department.

12. Variables or measures exist which when monitored indicate the success or failure of activities.

13. Measures include indicators of what the institution considers important.

14. Processes are considered multidimensional (happen over time, have sequential functions, involve multiple personnel, etc.) and are integrated with participants' beliefs.

15. External events are associated with internal activities.

16. Success in key areas can be monitored or recognized by observable events.

17. Decision making is considered by most campus officials to be part of a logical decision making process.

18. Variables are selected after reviewing literature, looking at previous institutional studies, and discussions with knowledgeable individuals.

19. There are visible relationships between goals, decisions, and rewards.

20. Offices and departments can describe their key success factors.

Collect and Store Data

1. Data element descriptions exist with enforced standards and extracted point-in-time census date databases.

2. There is a list of the various entities which are described in the databases.

3. For each entity, there is a master list of attributes to include at least the long name, short name, abbreviation, code/ID number, and database location.

4. For each attribute, in the definition, there is a short description, standard name, source, storage location, allowable categories, type of element, length and type of field, date last updated, responsible individual (custodian), reference and reporting requirements, valid values and edit checks, and archiving requirements.

5. There are extract databases for managerial and strategic use along with operational databases for functional activities.

6. The access process is documented for each element.

7. The information about information is accessible and understandable.

8. There are standard procedures for extracting, editing, auditing, merging, and altering data.

9. The data systems are useful for various groups of individuals; both strategic and operational users.

10. Databases are flexible and usable in various environments and they are simple and easy to use.

11. A data element dictionary is readily available to data analysts and data users.

12. Responsibility for data is assigned to key administrators (custodians) who are evaluated on their support of this responsibility.

13. Data are captured as near to the source point as possible and audited for allowable codes as it is entered.

14. Administrative Systems and Services Group(s) coordinate databases and user needs.

15. Relevant data elements are extracted from the operating systems, integrated and put into a census file.

16. Data from various multiple academic periods can be merged into a single file.

17. "Should be" data elements are reviewed for possible change.

18. Read/write security is consistent with managerial responsibility.

19. Requests for new systems and computers require compatibility with local standards.

20. The policy for managing data exists and has been revised in the last two years.

Restructure and Analyze Facts

1. Flow charting the information process exists and reflects the flow chart of the decision process.

2. Written procedures for restructuring and recoding data are available to analysts.

3. There is a set of procedures/standards for extracting and merging data from databases inside AND outside the institutional research office.

4. Data flows and analyses are audited and corrections are documented.

5. Definitions exist for complex concepts based on combinations of basic data values.

6. Those who analyze the data are trained in and use standard packages. Advisory groups of faculty are formed for specific projects of a technical nature.

7. User groups exist and contain users, analysts, and technicians for major databases.

8. Measures are interpretable and users understand what the codes really mean.

9. Procedures used to summarize and synthesize data are understood and results can be interpreted.

10. The sequences of events in the physical process represented by the data are documented.

11. Some of the information users are ex-analysts.

12. Those who analyze the data have a personal knowledge of the processes by which the data are captured.

13. After the initial capture of the data, only value-added transactions occur.

14. Administrators have analytic perspectives and computer confidence.

15. Users can integrate distributed census-date databases using office technology.

16. Analyses use multiple measures and where possible adjust for various conditions, which occur while the students are enrolled, such as changing the institutional calendar.

17. Combinations of methods are used to look at the results from several perspectives.

18. The data are analyzed with a focus on the concerns and the capabilities of the users.

19. Where possible, definitions are used which are consistent with external reports.

20. Graphic and descriptive methods are used effectively and can be replicated.

Deliver and Report Information

1. Systematic procedures are used to identify those for whom the information is appropriate and authorized.

2. The delivery systems and documentation is at the level of the users' ability.

3. Data are in systems or warehouses where statistics can be computed in an easy manner.

4. State, federal, and local reporting is ongoing, somewhat automated, and refined as an ongoing process.

5. Reporting encourages dealing with real problems and not working just to find fault or "improving" the numbers.

6. The degree to which the results can be generalized to various groups is determined as part of the process and explained in available documentation.

7. Results of studies are integrated into the standard information systems of the college.

8. Processes and information flows are used to implicitly or explicitly manage the relationships with key stakeholders.

9. Results of studies and various key data are distributed to the various committees of the college.

10. Strategies are used to disseminate the information in a manner consistent with the need.

11. Standard graphic and analysis packages are used and are generally available.

12. A calendar of key decision dates is available to technicians and reviewed periodically.

13. Periodic reports are in a standard format.

14. Reports tell users the extent to which results can be generalized.

15. There are centrally coordinated standard networks, e-mail, and data handling tools.

16. Reports from various groups on the same topics have the same numbers.

17. Results are not heavily influenced by the methodology or measures used to obtain them.

18. Results support ability to attribute outcomes to specific causes.

19. Results of analyses reflect reality and generalize to other groups and future situations.

20. There are resources on campus for those who want to learn to use the information system.

Use and Influence Decisions

1. Members of the faculty use the information system.

2. Users see the information as unbiased and reputable, analysts are considered ethical.

3. Special requests are grouped into a periodic report and decisions are moved from unstructured to structured decisions.

4. Key administrators often meet with those who provide the data and those who do the analyses.

5. Vice Presidents and the President make frequent use of the information.

6. Information providers include those who share the values of higher education and who understand the management of the college or university.

7. Rational decision making procedures are used and based on data, ideas, and personal experiences.

8. Unanswered questions are part of every decision.

9. There are systematic reviews of information adequacy after major events.

10. Users come looking for late reports.

11. Problems are solved as part of a joint learning process, not as responses to unconnected emergencies.

12. Linkage and dialogue are established among the suppliers, producers, and users of assessment results.

13. Opportunities are provided for meaningful interaction among those who develop, manage, and use institutional databases so that there are numerous opportunities to detect and correct system errors.

14. Appropriate evaluation activities are identified at the institutional and department/program levels; responsibilities at each level are assigned to provide adequate support.

15. There are established priorities that insure existing databases are developed.

16. Information is organized around issues or problems that the institution is committed to addressing.

17. Findings are summarized so that the "bottom line" is easily reached by those who are less than enamored with the detail required by scientific methodology.

18. Adequate information is available to support decision making before the opportunity to decide has passed.

19. Baseline data are established and targets are set so that expectations of results are realistic.

20. A routine mechanism is developed for reviewing results and recommending use.

Summary:

Function	Iden/Mea	Col/Stor	Restr/An	Deliv/Rep	Use/Infl	Total
Score						

REFERENCES

AIR Newsletter, September 14, 1992. Original source lost in antiquity.

Alter, S. (1991). Information systems: a management perspective. Reading, Massachusetts: Addison-Wesley.

Balkan, L., McLaughlin, G. W. (1992). A new data management culture for our new organizations. Paper presented at Data Administration Management Association Annual Meeting.

Balkan, L., McLaughlin, G. W., & Harper, B. (1992). Building the standards foundation for quality information from distributed systems. CAUSE/EFFECT, Winter, pp.33-34.

Balkan, L., & Sheldon, P. (1990). Developing guidelines for IRM: a grassroots process in a decentralized environment. CAUSE/EFFECT, V. 13, Summer, pp. 25-33.

Balkan, L., McLaughlin, G. W., & Howard, R. D. (1992). Distributed data management: people processes that build quality. Proceedings of the 1992 National CAUSE Conference.

Data Administration Management Association (DAMA) (1993). Manual for data administration. In J. J. Newton, & D. G. Wald, (Eds). NIST Special Publication 500-208. Gathersburg, Maryland: NIST.

Deal, T. E., & Kennedy, A. A. (1982). Corporate cultures: the rites and rituals of corporate life. Reading, Massachusetts: Addison-Wesley.

Durell, W. R. (1985). Data administration: a practical guide to successful data administration. New York, New York: McGraw-Hill.

Drucker, P. F. (1985). Innovation and entrepreneurship. New York, New York: Harper and Row.

Geller, E. S. (1989). Applied behavior analysis and social marketing: an integration for environmental preservation. Journal of Social Issues, V. 45, No. 1, pp. 17-36.

Gitlow, Howard S. and Gitlow, Shelly J. (1987).The Deming guide to quality and competitive position. Englewood Clifts, NJ: Prentice-Hall, Inc.

Goodhue, Kirsch, Quillard, & Wybo (1992). Strategic data planning: lessons from the field. MIS Quarterly, p. 25.

Hackathorn, R. (1995). Data warehousing energizes your enterprise. Datamation, pp. 38-45.

Harper, S. C. (1992). The challenges facing CEOs, past, present, and future. The Executive, V. VI, No. 3, pp. 10-11.

Howard, R. D., McLaughlin, G. W., & McLaughlin, J. S. (1989). Bridging the gap between the database and user in a distributed environment. CAUSE/EFFECT, V. 12, Summer, pp. 19-25.

Inmon, W. H. (1993). Building the data warehouse. Boston, Massachusetts: QED Publishing Group.

King, B. (1989). Better designs in half the time. Methuen, Massachusetts: GOAL/QPC.

Kubler-Ross, E. (1974). Questions and answers on death and dying. New York, New York: McMillan.

McLaughlin, G. W., & McLaughlin, J. S. (1989). Barriers to information use: the organizational context in enhancing information use in decision making. In P. T. Ewell(ED.), New directions in institutional research, No. 64, San Francisco, California: Jossey-Bass.

McLaughlin, G. W. & Howard, R. D. (1991). Check the quality of your information support. CAUSE/EFFECT, V. 14, Spring, pp. 23-27.

McLaughlin, G. W., Teeter, D. J., Howard, R. D., & Schots, J. S. (1987). The influence of policies on data use. CAUSE/EFFECT, January, pp. 6-10.

Merlyn, V. (1992). The critical few. Information Week, October, p. 40.

Miles, M. B., & Huberman, A. M. (1994). Qualitative data analysis. Thousand Oaks, California: SAGE Publications.

Mintzberg, H. (1973). The nature of managerial work. Englewood Cliffs, New Jersey: Prentice-Hall.

Miselis, K. L. (1990). Organizing for information resource management in organizing effective institutional research offices. In J. B. Presley (ED.), New directions for institutional research. San Francisco, California: Jossey-Bass.

Peck, M. S. (1987). The different drummer—community making and peace. New York, New York: Simon & Schuster, Inc.

Plice, S. J. (1992). Changing the culture: implementing TQM in an IT organization. CAUSE/EFFECT, Summer, p. 23.

Radding, A. (1992). Quality is job #1. Datamation, October, p. 100.

Rifkin, J. with Howard, T. (1981). Entropy: a new world view. New York, New York: Bantam Books.

Rockart, J. F., & DeLong, D. W. (1988). Executive support systems. Homewood, Illinois: DowJones-Irwin.

Senge, P. (1990). The fifth discipline. New York, New York: Currency Doubleday.

Silverman, D. (1993). Interpreting qualitative data. Thousand Oaks, California: SAGE Publications.

Simon, H. A. (1983). Methods of bounded rationality. V. 2, Boston, Massachusetts: MIT Press.

Stares, A., & Corbin, J. (1990). Basics of qualitative research. Newbury Park, California: Sage Publications.

Stringer, R. A. with Uchenick, J. L. (1986) Strategy traps and how to avoid them. Lexington, Massachusetts: Lexington Books.

Tapscott, D. (1992). The paradigm shift. Information Week. New York, New York: McGraw-Hill.

Tasker, D. (1998, February 6). IBM repository on its way. Computerworld, 87-90.

The Rise of Managerial Computing. (1986). In J. F. Rockart, & C. V. Bullen, (Eds.), Homewood, Illinois: Dow Jones-Irwin.

Tzu, S. (1971). The art of war. Translated by Samuel B. Griffith. New York, New York: Oxford University Press.

Waldrop, M. M. (1993). Complexity: the emerging science at the edge of order and chaos. New York, New York: Simon and Schuster.

Readings in information systems: a managerial perspective. (1988). In J. C. Wetherbe, V. T. Dock, & S. L. Mandell, (Eds.), St. Paul, Minnesota: West Publishing Co.

Wurman, R. S. (1990). Information anxiety. New York, New York: Bantam Books.